What did you *really* do today?

A Fresh Look at Time Management

By Peter Kennard FInstSMM

What did you really do today? – A Fresh Look at Time Management

First published in Great Britain in 2014

This edition published in 2014

All rights reserved. No part of this publication may be reproduced, stored on a retrieval system, or transmitted in any form or by any means, electronic, mechanical, photocopying, recording, or otherwise, without the express prior written permission of the copyright owner.

ISBN number 9781 849 145 930

Discover more at www.petekennardtraining.co.uk

What did you really do today? – A Fresh Look at Time Management

How to use this book

This is not your average book about time management. Rather, in writing it I have intended to create a hybrid textbook / workbook, where you read a few pages at a time and then reflect and implement relevant elements from the section just covered before moving on.

This means that the book will take somewhat longer than normal to complete, but that because it will be consumed in 'bite-sized chunks' it should result in incremental changes being made that are more likely to become permanent.

It is important to say that there is no single blueprint for managing one's time effectively. If there was, somebody would have published it and we'd all be doing it already! What works for one person may not be appropriate for the next, even where the two are colleagues in the same department and perhaps even doing a similar job, and thus individuals should seek approaches that they are comfortable with and which suit their working style.

With the last point in mind, think of this book as a 'buffet' of ideas. Take what you like, leave what you don't, and try some of the things that you've not tried before!

Good luck and I hope you enjoy the 'journey' towards greater personal effectiveness.

Pete Kennard

What did you really do today? – A Fresh Look at Time Management

Contents

The content of this publication is divided into sections shown below as days ('day one', 'day two' etc.). It is not essential that the book is completed in as little as 16 days, but it is recommended that you stop after each section and review your current practices, undertaking the specified activities and implementing any changes that seem appropriate immediately, <u>and</u> before moving on to the next section. Approaching the book in this way should allow you to build changes into your working patterns a bit at a time that collectively result in permanent and very real benefits.

At the end of the book there is a glossary of terms, which should serve as both a reference point and reminder of some of the key elements of personal effectiveness.

Page	Title
	Day one
7	Introduction
9	Personal objectives
10	Back to 'square one'
13	Where to start
	Day two
16	My job
18	Am I a creature of habit?
20	How much time can be saved?
	Day three
22	Concentration levels and attention spans
24	Prime time
26	Personal energy cycle

What did you really do today? – A Fresh Look at Time Management

	Day four
31	Prioritising
35	Planning your time
37	Time planning aids
	Day five
42	Daily planner (example)
43	Filing systems
	Day six
47	Your working environment
	Day seven
53	Managing interruptions
57	Assertiveness and time management
	Day eight
60	Meetings
	Day nine
67	Delegation
70	Motivation
	Day ten
75	Deal with things only once!
	- Deal with it
	- Delegate it
	- Schedule it
	- File it
	- Bin it
	Day eleven
78	Reading
80	Writing
	Day twelve
84	E-mail and mobile devices
	Day thirteen
91	Travel
96	Waiting time

©2014 Pete Kennard

	Day fourteen
98	Core time management principles
99	Change and time management
	Day fifteen
104	Time management ideas tips
	Day sixteen
120	Time quotes
	Day seventeen
122	One month later
	Glossary of terms
125	A to Z glossary of common time management terms
	About the author
129	Further information about the author

What did you really do today? – A Fresh Look at Time Management

Introduction

Some years ago people would have laughed at the thought of *me* writing a book about time management as my name was synonymous with the proverbial 'headless chicken'! But, as I increasingly heard the phrase "you're not getting any younger Pete", my approach to the subject began to alter and I started to look for and implement changes that made a positive difference to my work life in particular (and my home life as a consequence).

However, the road to becoming more effective was not an easy one and there were several 'false starts' along the way. The first mistake I made was to seek only initiatives that would save huge chunks of time, and I quickly became disappointed. I discovered that, whilst there is usually scope for improvement in some areas, most of these appear to have been 'done' already!

Another error was to assume that I already knew how I was actually spending my days, and it was only after making a time log that I realised my best-laid plans were often punctuated with far more interruptions than I would ever have believed. But I guess the thing that almost stopped me altogether was the fact that, even after reading books, watching films and attending training courses on the subject, any discernible improvements seemed small and relatively short-lived. In other words and metaphorically-speaking, the payback wasn't normally worth the investment.

It also quickly became apparent to me that there are a lot of myths about time management which can derail those with the best of intentions, as well as a good number of blunt truths and simple concepts that, if embraced, can be enormously beneficial. Unfortunately, most of the former are quite well known (and in some cases even well documented), and thus it may be necessary to first 'unlearn' some of these before we can make meaningful and long-lasting changes.

What did you really do today? – A Fresh Look at Time Management

So I decided to take my experiences and share them in a way that is perhaps a little different from other books on the subject. Specifically, this is not a publication that is intended to be read quickly; indeed it should be read in short bursts with a gap between one section and the next in order to afford the reader the opportunity to reflect and try to implement any of the ideas that he / she feels may be helpful. This way, they might just 'stick'!

It is also acknowledged from the outset that good time management is, by definition, a very personal thing and that a 'one size fits all' approach would be futile. Jobs, responsibilities, pressures, working styles and colleagues can all impact on how effective we are, and thus what works for person 'A' might well be impossible to implement (or even counter-productive) for person 'B'.

And are we looking for the same goal in terms of improved time management anyway? The motivation for example may be to become more organised, to schedule / plan more effectively, take a lunch break, say "no" to unreasonable demands, prevent procrastination, reduce stress levels, or improve one's work-life balance, though of course these are not mutually exclusive, as very often several will be closely linked.

So if you can relate to any of this then please read on, and we'll share a journey together that should result in better time management and improved effectiveness in the long-term.

What did you really do today? – A Fresh Look at Time Management

Personal objectives

Everybody has different 'goals' in terms of their time management. Consider the list below, and indicate those areas you would like to improve. (The blank box at the bottom is for you to add any specific objectives of your own).

Factor	Very significant	Quite significant	Not significant
Day-to-day planning (e.g. prioritising, goal setting, completing tasks, lists etc.)			
Planning and executing medium and long-term activities (e.g. projects)			
Distinguishing between urgent and important tasks, and scheduling			
Balancing work and private time, and being able to 'switch off'			
Being able to say "no" politely, resisting interruptions and managing workloads			
Delegating / letting go			
Reviewing processes and finding more efficient ways of doing things			
Making 'value judgements' and arriving at appropriate decisions			
Communicating effectively with others, particularly in the written medium			
Working to deadlines (without rushing to finish)			
Personal time-keeping (being in control of what needs doing when)			

©2014 Pete Kennard

What did you really do today? – A Fresh Look at Time Management

Back to 'square one'

Whilst time itself may be infinite, the amount that you or I have is most definitely finite! In other words (and to quote a well-known UK supermarket chain) "once it's gone it's gone".

But despite the fact that this resource is quite literally 'ticking away', few of us seem to value it fully. Benjamin Franklin was credited with the quote "time is money" and I wonder if we started thinking of time in financial terms whether it would become a higher priority for us?

Very often people talk of others wasting or even stealing their time (the term 'time-thieves' is much used in this context) and it seems that we sometimes allow or even invite this, but that we probably wouldn't take such a liberal view of the same person 'dipping in' to our wallet or purse and taking out a couple of tenners!

Consider this scenario for a moment; if a dozen people are at a meeting and (for whatever reason) the meeting starts just five minutes late then it's not just five minutes that have been wasted but one hour *collectively* that has been lost! Similarly missing the post by just one minute could make a difference of 24 hours or more if the item now arrives at its destination on the following day, with who-knows-what in the way of knock-on consequences for the recipient(s).

So our starting point has to be to think about time differently. Since it can't be manufactured we must consider it a limited resource, at least from a personal perspective, and cherish it appropriately. It doesn't matter who you are, there are just 168 hours available to you per week, and roughly one third of those can immediately be discounted to allow for sleep.

What did you really do today? – A Fresh Look at Time Management

And it's not just about being busy either (because we can probably all lay claim to that one), it's *what we're busy at* that matters. There really is a difference between being busy and being effective, and good time management is not about activity, it's about achievement.

Good time management is also about 'opportunity cost', that is to say considering what else we might be doing with that chunk of our day were we not doing what we have chosen to do, and thinking about whether the alternative(s) might be more appropriate or beneficial.

One of the biggest challenges is that a lot of what people (and in some cases organisations) do is born out of habit. Ask *why* something is done in a particular way and the response will quite often be "we've always done it like that". To be fair, most of us do a lot of things out of routine and very often these routines have come about after trying alternatives that have proven to be less successful. But the problem is that once a method that works has been established, many of us adopt the "if it isn't broken don't fix it" mentality, and with the passage of years, whilst it may not be 'broken' as such it may nonetheless become less fit for purpose!

There is a popular saying that goes something like "if all you ever do is all you've ever done, then all you'll ever have is all you've ever had". Now some may argue that there is nothing wrong with that, especially if everything is satisfactory at the moment, but the fact is that change is inevitable and that methods that may seem appropriate or even 'cutting edge' today may become out-dated and ineffective relatively quickly.

Take for example travel, technology, communication or leisure. All are constantly evolving, and to remain the same actually has the effect of regressing rather than maintaining the status-quo, meaning that the quote at the start of the previous paragraph should more accurately read "if all you ever do is all you've ever done, you'll probably end up with less than you had and others will overtake you"! Thus our effectiveness is at serious risk of erosion unless we are both receptive to new ideas and prepared to review our ways every so often.

What did you really do today? – A Fresh Look at Time Management

The default is that if we don't make decisions about our time then somebody else probably will! Put simply, others will take advantage if we allow them to do so, and the management of our time will be controlled, or at least seriously influenced, by third parties. Being able to say "no" is important if we are to be 'masters of our own destiny', and effectively managing time also requires competency in areas such as assertiveness, communication and negotiation skills.

Some years ago a former employer warned me that it doesn't pay to be overly helpful at work, especially where the assistance you are providing is outside the remit of your role. The phrase that he used, and that has stuck in my mind since is "once is a favour, twice a habit, and three times it's now your job"! At the time I probably didn't realise the significance of what he was saying, but many of us pick up 'baggage' as we spend longer in our roles; some to the extent that they probably wouldn't recognise their own job description if it didn't contain their job title!

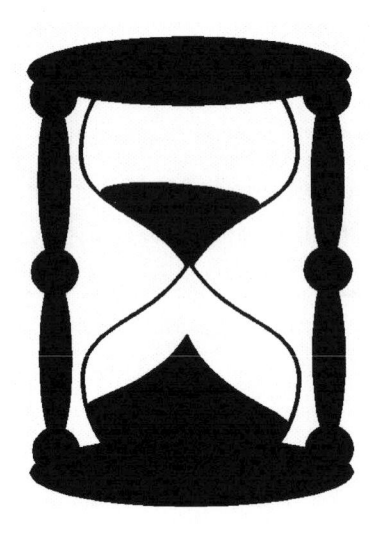

What did you really do today? – A Fresh Look at Time Management

Where to start

Ironically, the first step on the road to becoming more effective will actually take a small amount of time, but it is a necessary activity upon which the foundations of better time management are built, so it cannot be avoided.

That first step is to make a time log of a typical working day, and you really must undertake this at the earliest opportunity.

The purpose of this activity is to establish exactly what you do, and literally everything should be recorded. That said it need not be that time-consuming in itself as forms of shorthand can be used, but do ensure that every task is recorded, together with every interruption and disruption etc., whether planned or not. It is also imperative that every entry in your log has a duration noted against it as this will enable you to calculate the proportion of your day that is being spent on particular activities, and also how your time is punctuated. Don't forget to include your comfort breaks too, as although the purpose is not to reduce these, unless you document them an accurate picture of how you spend your day cannot be established.

How you choose to record the information is entirely up to you and will be influenced by the nature of work that you do, but as a minimum you will need to include columns for the following:

- Task / activity
- Start time (and duration or possibly end time)
- Did you plan to do it now (Y/N)?
- Were you interrupted (Y/N or tally)?
- Comments

What did you really do today? – A Fresh Look at Time Management

If this is done properly it is likely that you will need several sheets as most people have dozens of entries on a properly completed log. It might be that the resulting document looks something like this:

Time Log: *Joe Bloggs*   **Date:** *20/02/14*   **Sheet:** *1 of 4*

Task	Start time (duration)	Planned now	Interrupted	Comments
Arrive at work	08.55			
Make coffee	08.58 (7 min's)	Yes	No	Chat with colleagues
Switch on PC	09.05 and wait for it to boot up	Yes	Yes (phone call*)	* Took message for Tom
Check e-mails	09.09 (23 min's)	Yes	Yes (boss stopped by to advise meeting at 09.30	14 new e-mail messages
Impromptu staff meeting	09.32 (26 min's)	No. Called by boss just now	N/A	I was 2 mins late for meeting
Sort inbound post	09.58 (33 min's)	Yes but would usually have started earlier	4 inbound phone calls (only 3 of which were for me**)	** Took message for Roger
Cigarette break	10.31 (11 min's)	Roughly		
Filing	10.42 (14 min's)	No	Asked to help with copier jam (6 mins)	Chatted with Jan re supplies

What did you really do today? – A Fresh Look at Time Management

TOP TIPS

- Make a time log so you know how you're currently spending your time, and how often and by what / who you're being interrupted.
- Check your work / life balance. Do you live to work, or work to live?
- Beware – if you don't control your time then somebody else will!

LOCK IT IN

You should now stop reading and not continue any further until you have completed your time log.

What did you really do today? – A Fresh Look at Time Management

My job

We all know why we go to work and what we're supposed to do right? Well, perhaps not. It's all too easy to become caught up on the 'treadmill' of working life and, if we're not careful, to lose sight of why we're there in the first place!

Imagine that you were being introduced for the first time to somebody who had absolutely no idea about your occupation or what your work involved. You would probably tell them your job title, offer a brief outline of your responsibilities, and explain how what you do affects others (or maybe the organisation).

From a time management perspective it can be very useful to think about this and actually write it down, as to do so can help with focus and prioritising (including delegating where appropriate). However, it is important to capture it in an accurate but succinct way, with the emphasis on the core elements of your role. Too vague and it will be of no use at all, and too long and it will be difficult to separate 'the wood from the trees'.

Component elements are therefore:

- Job title
- Responsibilities (overview)
- Key outcomes

For example, *the Data Entry Clerk* (job title) *is responsible for prompt and accurate entry of financial statistics on spread-sheets* (main responsibilities) *so that senior managers can access information enabling them to identify trends in spending and make budgetary decisions for the company* (outcomes).

What did you really do today? – A Fresh Look at Time Management

Another might read *the Training Co-ordinator* (job title) *is responsible for collating development requests and conducting a quarterly training needs analysis* (main responsibilities) *so that staff have the appropriate up-to-date knowledge and skills in order to undertake their jobs safely and effectively* (outcomes).

Or *the Store Manager* (job title) *is responsible for stock control, staffing, and retail displays* (main responsibilities) *so that the branch hits its sales targets and contributes to the overall profitability of the region* (outcomes).

Note that in each case the responsibilities and outcomes are deliberately stated quite broadly so as to avoid becoming 'bogged down' with specific tasks, and that they aim to capture the primary purpose(s) of the role. Similar wording is sometimes found on one's job description under headings such as 'Role Purpose' or 'Context', or in advertisements for job vacancies where employers try to 'paint a picture' of what the position is all about.

Now try to construct a sentence in the same format as the examples above that describes your role. Once you are happy with it, write it in the space below.

What did you really do today? – A Fresh Look at Time Management

Am I a creature of habit?

The previous activity (capturing the essence of your role in a single sentence including job title, key responsibilities and primary outcomes) can be quite a tricky one as many people tend to become conditioned in terms of what they do regularly. This means that very often they don't revisit *why* things are being done in a particular way, at a particular time, or in a particular order, or perhaps the priority that specific tasks are being given.

Such an approach allows individuals to operate in 'autopilot' mode with the pre-conscious part of their brain taking care of these habitual or repetitive actions. Whilst this may be a safe way of doing things (i.e. it seemed to work okay last time so I'll do it that way again as it is, by definition, proven) it lacks the validity checks that effective time management demands.

Every so often a good time manager will check to see whether these routines are still the best way of doing things, and be prepared to both 'think outside the box' and make changes where they could be beneficial. It is worth adding that not all of these alterations will necessarily work first time and that you may occasionally have to revert to previous ways, but unless new approaches are at least tested every so often it is likely that you will become less effective over time.

The majority of people, when asked, will say that they are not 'creatures of habit'. However, the same people may admit to parking the car in their 'normal' space (or area) in a car park, or visiting the supermarket on a specific day and time each week and then travelling the aisles in the same order. Likewise they may change the bedding on a Monday or cut the grass on a Saturday but when challenged as to *why*, may struggle to justify this. Equally, many people feel irritated when their routines are disrupted. For example when the area of the car park is full or the supermarket decides to move everything around (which they do, incidentally, because they know that customers may miss some of their products because of the routine nature of their shopping).

What did you really do today? – A Fresh Look at Time Management

Often individuals become quite defensive of their habits when asked to explain the rationale behind their actions. For example the commuter asked why he / she stands on the same section of the platform each and every morning may reply "why not?" adding that "everybody else does it". Indeed he / she is probably right, but it might be prudent for people to challenge themselves every so often to verify that what they are doing remains fully fit for purpose, and to test alternatives every now and then.

If we make choices out of habit away from the workplace then it is likely that we'll do so at work too. As I'll make clearer later on, the regular staff meeting, always opening the post as soon as it arrives, allowing e-mails to accumulate in your 'in box', and even having a second chair in the vicinity of your desk can all negatively impact on our time management.

Consider an average day from the second you wake up to the moment you go to bed and think about how many things you do routinely or out of habit.

What did you really do today? – A Fresh Look at Time Management

How much time can be saved?

In the same way that time cannot be manufactured, neither can it be 'saved'. It can, however, be *spent* much more productively!

At first glance the statement above might sound rather pedantic, but the terminology here is important if we are to fully understand what is meant by good time management.

But whilst time cannot be 'banked', it is perhaps worth pausing for a moment to consider the impact of changing our ways. I recall a conversation with my manager many years ago as part of an appraisal review that I was having at the time. He had identified (and I had agreed) that there was scope for me to become more effective and we were discussing specific techniques / changes that might benefit me. At the end of the discussion he asked me how much time I thought might be saved were I to implement the ideas we had talked about and, not wishing to over commit myself (or to appear as though I had been slacking in the past) I answered his question somewhat guardedly. "I guess", I said, "that if I do everything we've discussed, then I might be able to do what I used to do in an hour in maybe 57 minutes"!

I was pleased with my rather non-committal reply and expected him to try to negotiate on the somewhat unimpressive saving that I had estimated. But instead of that he replied "that's great Pete … saving three minutes an hour is the equivalent of saving two and a half weeks a year".

And of course he was right. Three minutes is one twentieth of an hour and two and a half weeks is one twentieth of a year, but I had never thought of it that way before. And he was right about another thing too, that being that the small savings really do add up! Indeed this was something of a 'Eureka moment' for me, and a point in my life when I started to take the subject of time management much more seriously.

What did you really do today? – A Fresh Look at Time Management

Previously I had always sought ideas that would save hours at a time, and generally looked scornfully at what I had regarded as tiny savings. But, as he also pointed out, these savings all add up. They are also generally very much easier to implement too, making them something of a 'win-win'!

"Look after the pennies and the pounds will look after themselves" is a well- known statement often attributed to the wise. Well I have just described the time management equivalent, and one that we would be unwise to disregard!

TOP TIPS

- Think about why your job exists. Maybe refer to your job description or role profile. Is there a close correlation between your regular activities and your responsibilities?
- Considering routine tasks particularly, reflect on why you undertake specific activities at certain times. Have you ever reviewed this?
- You can't 'save' time, but you may be able to spend it more productively.
- Don't disregard the small time savings; they all add up!

LOCK IT IN

You should now stop reading for today. Check that you have written a sentence that describes your role (page 17), and think about the cumulative effect that any small changes may have on your personal effectiveness and how you might use that 'extra' time.

Concentration levels and attention spans

This book is deliberately intended to be read in short bursts so that readers don't become fatigued and so that ideas and suggestions can be introduced bit by bit. But most people have sat in a meeting at one time or another and 'drifted off', or read a report only to find that they have reached the bottom of the page and have no idea what it was all about. Maybe you have watched a film and found the time to be 'dragging', or perhaps have had to ask your partner to repeat something that they've just said to you?

Of course such occurrences are quite normal but clearly if we are missing things, or for that matter having to duplicate them because of spells of inattention, these are areas we must consider and correct if we are to truly operate effectively.

There are few generic 'rules of thumb' when it comes to concentration and attention, except to say that generally it is a good idea to mix less and more appealing tasks together rather than leaving all of the 'nasty' ones until last, to make sure that no single activity lasts for too long, and to ensure that you take regular breaks in order to 'recharge those batteries'.

Everything else is personal with relevant factors including to what extent the task motivates us, how varied / challenging the work is, the length of time since our last break, the environment, proximity to others, noise levels, our health, time of day, tiredness, workload, stress and other matters on our mind.

Some Americans refer to 'chunking' large tasks, that is to say breaking them down into smaller pieces. This has the dual benefit of making them easier to schedule in to our diaries and also making them seem less daunting (or relatively more appealing).

What did you really do today? – A Fresh Look at Time Management

A great deal of research has been undertaken in the area of concentration levels and attention spans and, whilst the numbers vary from study to study, most agree that working through rest periods is largely counter-productive. The main reason for this is that the fatigue felt later in the day often slows people to the extent that the net level of achievement is no greater than it would have been had that individual stopped and taken a break in the first place. Indeed sometimes less is achieved overall, and certainly where the person is working in a hazardous environment it is likely that he / she may not be as attentive and thus at greater risk as a consequence.

Human beings are not machines and need regular rest and sustenance in order to perform at the 'top of their game'. Some schools have introduced bottled water for their students claiming that it aids concentration, whilst the benefits of 'power napping' and the rules around hours for drivers of larger and public service vehicles are well known for obvious reasons.

So the message is that people should build rest periods into their schedules and that they should guard against these being eroded. The schedule, wherever possible, should take account of other factors likely to keep the worker 'fresh' as they will probably complete their tasks more quickly overall and with greater accuracy. The smart worker is not the one who puts in the most hours; rather the one who uses their time most effectively.

What did you really do today? – A Fresh Look at Time Management

Prime time

Now here's a question for you. If you could 'ring-fence' say an hour a day where you were guaranteed to have total silence and be completely un-interrupted, what would you use it for and do you think you would achieve more than in the same amount of time under standard work conditions?

I suspect that the answer to the second part of the question is probably "yes", and in fact some people effectively try to achieve this by either starting work earlier than their colleagues or staying on after normal hours, many citing "I get so much more done when nobody else is around and the 'phone isn't constantly ringing" as their justification. But the fact that this happens at all proves that with fewer interruptions people can be more productive, and begs the question whether (with the co-operation of others) a similar outcome could be achieved?

Of course some organisations have recognised the value of this and have allocated 'quiet rooms' in their offices, but even these are useless unless others respect them and everybody's entitlement to some un-interrupted time.

So the concept of 'prime time' was developed and this is already working successfully in a number of top businesses in the UK. The principle is very straightforward and simply needs colleague co-operation and a recognition that everybody could benefit from a little peace and quiet on a regular basis.

Where it has been established, it works something like this. Everybody is allowed say 45 minutes of prime time every day. During this period the individual(s) in question move away from their normal place of work to a quiet area, taking with them any significant work that is most at risk from error or delay where there are distractions and / or interruptions are likely. Examples of such activities might include report writing, dealing with complex issues,

What did you really do today? – A Fresh Look at Time Management

preparations for important meetings and suchlike. During this time, colleagues field any calls and deal with any issues as if the person was not in the building at all.

With this type of co-operation, the 'burden' on the remaining colleagues is shared and is no greater than if the person was at lunch, but the benefit to the individual using the prime time can be huge. And of course because prime time should be a reciprocal arrangement, that is to say everybody is entitled to the same amount of it irrespective of job title, time-served or seniority, people are usually reasonably happy to 'chip in and do their bit' in the knowledge that they too will have an opportunity to benefit.

If your workplace adopted the idea of prime time, what sort of activities would you use it for (these should be tasks that are most at risk of disruption in the normal run of events)? Make a note of your thoughts below.

Personal energy cycle

Over the years I have delivered dozens of courses on time management and have also discussed issues of effectiveness with hundreds of people as part of other training programmes. But sadly, whilst some people are happy to 'give it a go', on many occasions I have listened to explanations as to why one idea or another wouldn't work for them, or how their situation is so unique that every initiative is futile.

My response is always the same, and that is to talk about personal energy because even if it is impossible to influence any other area of time management (and frankly, I doubt that is the case – but more of that later!), one's personal energy cycle can *always* be used to good effect.

Your personal energy cycle is all about when you feel at your sharpest or most alert and when you don't. Few people can perform at 100% physically or mentally throughout the working day, and most of us experience peaks and troughs. Sometimes there is an obvious explanation for this variation in energy levels and sometimes there is not, but usually there is a pattern.

Once again (as so often seems to be the case) there is not a 'one size fits all' approach and it is necessary to think about how you work best in order to gain maximum benefit.

Thus the idea behind personal energy cycles is to first recognise when these peaks and troughs occur (for you as an individual because they may be different from those around you), and then to match your tasks according to your energy level at the time. This way you schedule high concentration tasks for times when you feel sharp and alert, and those less-demanding activities for periods where you are less so. This works because the high concentration tasks can be completed more quickly when you are alert, whereas the less demanding ones take approximately the same amount of time however you are feeling. If you think back to the previous section, it might also influence when you take your prime time too!

What did you really do today? – A Fresh Look at Time Management

Naturally some people have more control over what they do and at what time they do it than others (with managers usually having the greatest flexibility of all) but even the most junior people in an organisation will usually have some scope for planning their time in that, provided their tasks are completed by the end of the day, then that's all that really matters. Where this is the case then it is of no significance whether you work on it at 2.00pm or 4.30pm as long as it's done!

With these points in mind and thinking about your own job, make a list of tasks that you are responsible for that require high levels of energy / concentration.

Now list those that require moderate levels of energy / concentration.

What did you really do today? – A Fresh Look at Time Management

And finally list those that can be achieved adequately during low periods of energy / concentration.

Having established the type of tasks that match particular levels of energy, it is now necessary to plot the energy cycle in the form of a graph. Please draw yours on the next page, with energy (%) on the vertical axis, and time on the horizontal axis.

What did you really do today? – A Fresh Look at Time Management

My Typical Personal Energy Cycle

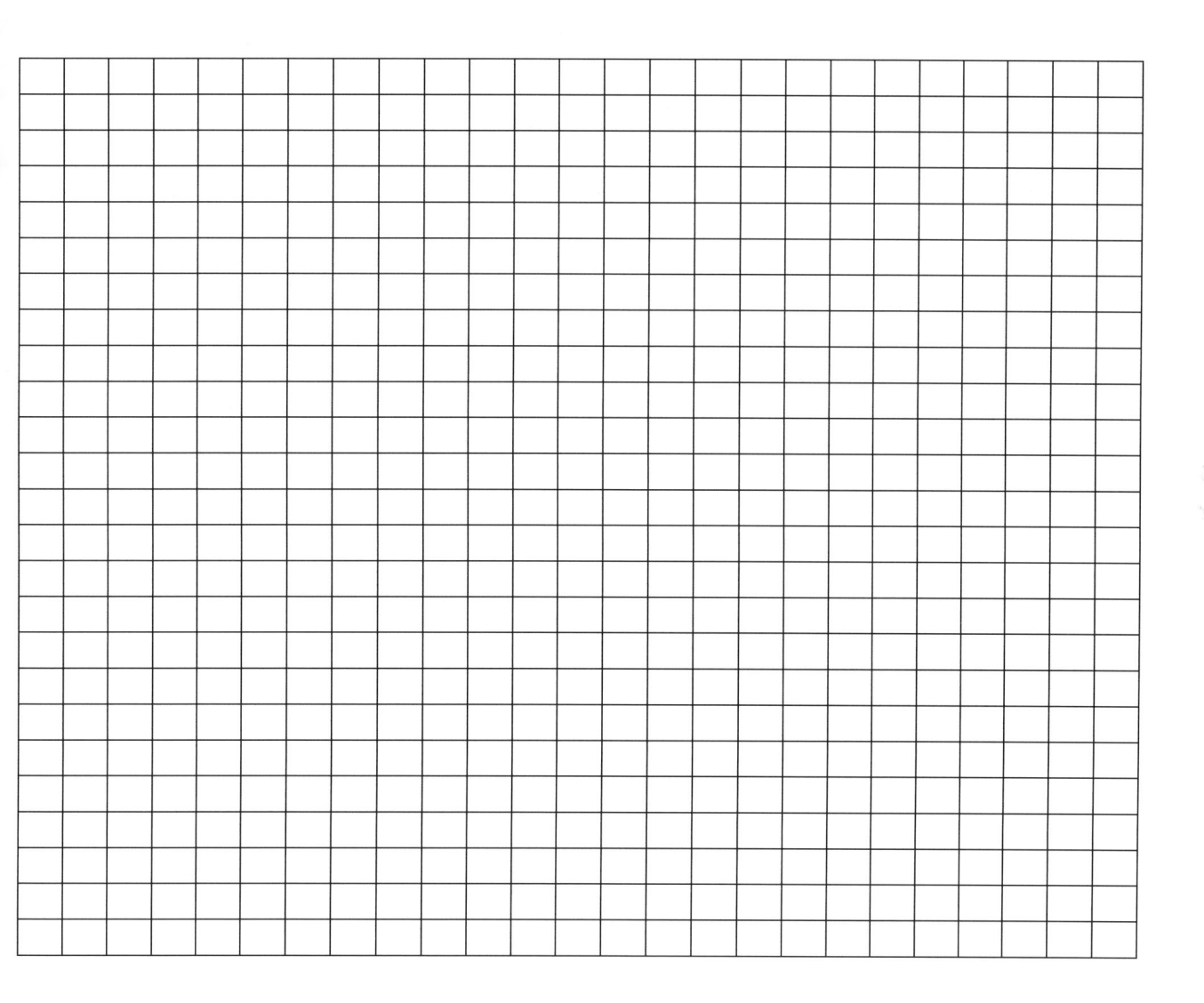

By now you should have identified typical peaks and troughs in your personal energy cycle and thought about scheduling your activities accordingly. Aim to plan for high concentration tasks to coincide with high-energy times, with less challenging activities undertaken where there are natural dips in energy levels.

What did you really do today? – A Fresh Look at Time Management

Be particularly cautious of regular mundane tasks that you are required to do at set times of day, especially where there is a mismatch in requirements and natural personal energy levels, and look to rearrange these where possible.

Finally, our metabolism is a factor that affects our personal energy cycle but it is worth adding that we can often influence it somewhat too, for example by doing our best to eat regularly and healthily and by taking exercise. Avoiding too much 'snacking', aiming for a balanced diet, and even using the stairs rather than taking the lift are all initiatives that can have a positive effect on our lives. The bottom line is that when we feel good we usually perform better.

TOP TIPS

- Think about 'chunking' (i.e. breaking down) larger tasks. This makes them easier to schedule in and also less daunting.
- Even if you're really busy, try not to skip too many breaks. You may not realise it but you will slow down if you don't take the chance to 'recharge your batteries'.
- Try to adopt the concept of 'prime time', if necessary working with colleagues to support each other in guarding against interruptions or distractions. Having done this, ensure that you make best use of the time.
- Consider your personal energy cycle, and ensure that (wherever possible) you take steps to match your energy levels with the demands of the task.

LOCK IT IN

- You should now stop reading for today. Check that you have documented how you would use your prime time, were the concept to be adopted in your place of work. Also, make sure that you have noted your high, medium and low energy / concentration tasks, and that you have plotted your typical workday energy cycle.

What did you really do today? – A Fresh Look at Time Management

Prioritising

An effective person will prioritise his / her work to maximise the likelihood of goals being met. But the concept of priorities is again a personal thing where what is deemed high priority for one person may not be as significant for the next.

To be able to prioritise properly, it is first necessary to establish whether the task / activity in question is *urgent* or *important* or both. These terms are central to effective planning but actually mean something very different from each other.

Urgency is a measure of time. In other words where something is urgent it needs doing soon (but not necessarily by you).

Importance on the other hand is a measure of consequence. Think of this as being consequence in relation to your role specifically. Put another way, if it is important then by definition it is something that is fundamentally your responsibility and that if it were not completed then the ramifications for you would be significant.

By and large importance does not change (unless you start a new job or your role profile is amended) as something either is your responsibility or it's not. However, urgency does change with the passage of time because where something has a deadline, the longer it is left uncompleted then the more urgent it becomes.

Understanding and appreciating the true meaning of these terms will allow you to prioritise your work, but will also help you to identify tasks / actions that can be delegated or even discontinued, so let us think about how this works in practice.

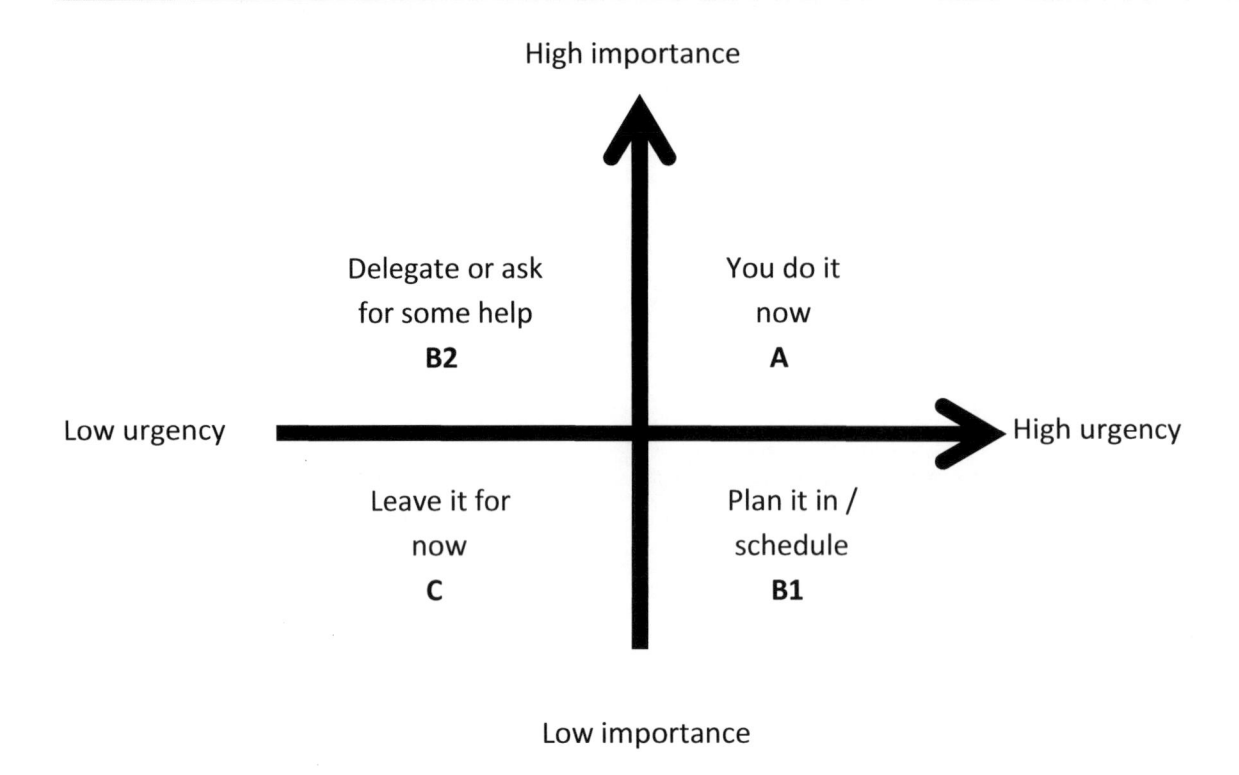

What did you really do today? – A Fresh Look at Time Management

```
                     High importance
                            ↑
                            |
      Delegate or ask       |    You do it
       for some help        |       now
           B2               |        A
                            |
Low urgency ————————————————+————————————————→ High urgency
                            |
       Leave it for         |    Plan it in /
           now              |      schedule
            C               |        B1
                            |
                     Low importance
```

The quadrants have been labelled A, B1, B2 and C.

Type A tasks are urgent and important and must be completed by you as soon as possible. It is likely that every day there will be some of these, but since you are effectively 'fire-fighting' or being reactive, you should take whatever steps you can to minimise their occurrence.

Type B tasks are either important or urgent but not both. They should account for the majority of your work and take up most of your day. Where possible focus on B1 tasks and delegate B2 tasks, as by definition the former are more significant for you albeit not as 'pressing' at that moment. If delegation is not an option for you then maybe consider asking for some help, or re-evaluating these activities to see whether somebody else should be doing them. Note that with time, incomplete B1 tasks will become type A tasks!

What did you really do today? – A Fresh Look at Time Management

Type C tasks are neither urgent nor important and can be left, at least for now, or done when time allows. However bear in mind that with the passage of time, if left undone, they may become type B2 tasks.

Now think about your role specifically. Basing your thoughts on what you *should be doing* rather than what you may be doing, make a list of your tasks against the prompts below.

List some of your tasks where you have a short lead-time (i.e. they have to be dealt with more or less on receipt).

✎

Now list some of your tasks where you are given plenty of notice (i.e. you can plan them in – please include holidays, scheduled meetings, training etc.).

✎

Now list tasks / activities which are wholly your responsibility and that are central to your role (refer to the definition of your role on page 17 if it helps).

✎

What did you really do today? – A Fresh Look at Time Management

Finally list some of those things that you get 'dragged into' or which are at best peripheral to your role.

Having done this, now plot some of your actual tasks on the grid below.

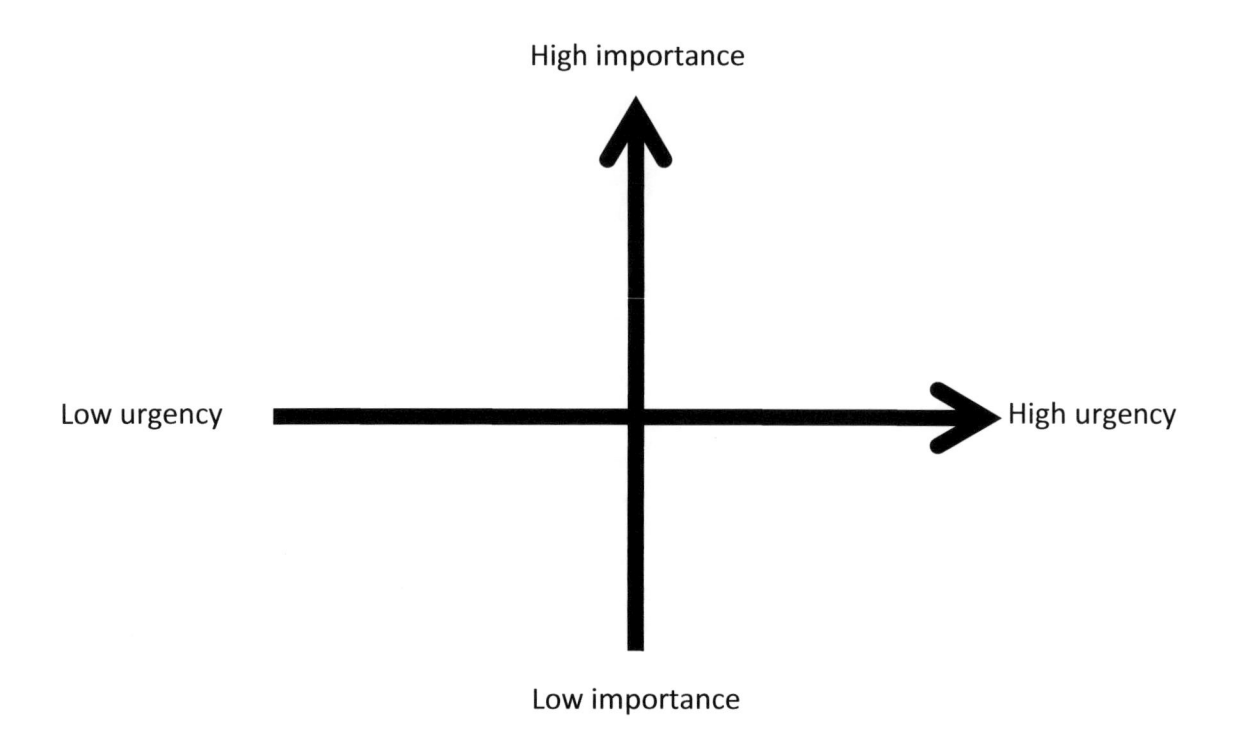

High importance

Low urgency ──────────────┼──────────────▶ High urgency

Low importance

What did you really do today? – A Fresh Look at Time Management

Planning your time

It is important to start each day, week and month with an idea of how you *intend* to utilise your time, and the old adage 'fail to plan, plan to fail' rings very true here since good time management is about being effective rather than simply busy.

But whilst it is a mistake not to plan, it can be equally counter-productive to create a schedule that is rigid to the extent that there is no space at all for contingencies. Filling every moment of every day just results in everything falling apart when the inevitable high priority (type A) tasks appear unexpectedly, with chaos often ensuing as there seems to be nowhere to fit them in!

So the trick is to strike a balance whereby type B1 tasks / activities are planned well in advance, but leaving at least some gaps so that you can 'fire-fight' the short-notice high important ones that are likely to crop up. Exactly how many gaps or how much time might be left for these tasks / activities will be determined by the nature of your work, but it should be possible to slot in those that would be genuinely problematic were they not addressed there and then.

If you manage other people it might also be prudent to allocate time in your schedule when team members or colleagues might talk with you. By doing this you can indicate to others that you are both busy and organised (at the same time educating them to think ahead before simply interrupting you without considering how disruptive this could be).

Within your scheduling remember to take account of your personal energy cycle and also consider how motivation might affect the relative speed at which one works. What I mean by this is that if you only plan mundane or unpleasant tasks for a lengthy period then it is more likely that your mind may wander (making you less effective as a consequence). So break up the less inspiring tasks so they don't follow one after another and try to maintain your productivity!

What did you really do today? – A Fresh Look at Time Management

In much the same way, large tasks that threaten to eat up huge amounts of time should be divided into smaller component parts. Breaking them down to their smallest denominator makes activities seem less daunting initially and also allows for greater flexibility when planning or moving things around. It may even highlight opportunities to delegate some elements to colleagues too! There is an old saying that asks: "Question – How do you eat an elephant? Answer – In bite sized chunks!"

Within your planning don't forget to schedule in some breaks, as unless you allow time to 'recharge your batteries' you will become gradually less effective as the day progresses. Think of this as a kind of preventative maintenance!

And finally when planning your time it is important to ensure that any objectives are SMART (Specific, Measurable, Achievable, Relevant and Timed), as failure to adhere to this mnemonic will inevitably result in a reduction in focus and a consequent loss of effectiveness.

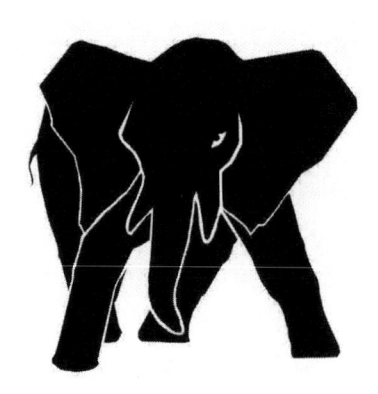

What did you really do today? – A Fresh Look at Time Management

Time planning aids

There is a plethora of supposed time management aids ranging from complex and expensive electronic organisers to a simple pencil and paper, but the best ones to use are those that suit your working style as these are the ones that you are most likely to keep up to date!

A simple 'To Do' list may be sufficient, though it is important to stress that in the real world everyone is likely to have to carry some tasks forward to the next day, so don't become downhearted if you don't complete it every day. Personally I prefer paper versions as they are very much 'in your face' and thus unlikely to be overlooked. There is also a certain satisfaction to be gained from actually crossing something off such a list (although there will of course also be things being added to it)!

A good 'To Do' list will have tasks noted together with some indication as to their priority (type A, B1, B2, or C) and it is good practice to ensure that you try to complete some B1 tasks daily in order that you don't become too reactive. Remember that type B1 tasks will become type A tasks if left for too long, and likewise that C's can become B2's.

Some people find that 'making appointments with their tasks' can help. This might seem like a strange concept at first glance, but essentially this is where one allocates a designated time period to undertake a specific piece of work. The idea is that larger tasks are actually written in the diary in much the same way as an appointment or a meeting would be, the rationale being that it focuses the mind about getting on with it. If the diary is visible (i.e. if it is a traditional paper diary rather than an online version) then it can also help reduce interruptions as others can actually see that you're busy. This approach is best used for planning type B1 activities and it is important to leave a few gaps so that there is some flexibility / contingency, and so that colleagues know when they may speak with you.

What did you really do today? – A Fresh Look at Time Management

Some people choose to set reminders on calendars on mobile phones, tablets and PCs etc. These can be very helpful if they are used correctly, but it seems that unfortunately many seem just to set a time to *start* tasks. The problem with this is that there is normally no warning that the designated time is approaching, and thus it can result in more 'fire-fighting'. If this is your preferred method then why not set the alarm for the beginning of that day or for say an hour before the task is due to commence? This way you can slot it in more appropriately and without too much panic.

Whiteboards for office-based workers can be useful as they are both visual and easily updated. But if you are mobile then maybe a tablet and stylus pen could achieve the same result?

Post-It™ notes are not usually helpful in planning one's own time as they tend to become lost and are quite messy when there are lots of them. This said, they are easily moveable and can be useful in group 'brainstorming' sessions, for 'chunking' larger projects into smaller more-manageable pieces, and for delegating type B2 and C tasks.

What methods do you currently use to plan your time (list all of them below)?

Could you utilise additional / alternative methods to help you become more effective at planning your time? If so, what might these be and how could they help you?

What did you really do today? – A Fresh Look at Time Management

If others (e.g. colleagues) were more aware of your priorities, do you think they would respect this and try not to disturb you unless absolutely necessary?

TOP TIPS

- In order to prioritise effectively, you must be able to distinguish between *urgent* and *important* tasks in relation to your role.
- Urgency is a measure of time, and importance relates to the consequences (for you) of not completing the task / activity.
- If it helps, use a grid to plot your tasks. Try to focus as much of your time as possible on the pro-active (B1) quadrant.
- Whilst it is a mistake not to plan, it can be equally counter-productive to over-plan. There must be some space and sufficient flexibility to be able to cope with the unexpected reactive situations that crop up.
- When scheduling your tasks, remember to take account of personal energy levels and motivation, as both may have a bearing on how long it will take to complete them.
- Ensure your objectives are SMART.
- Use time planning aids that suit your work and working style.
- Use a 'To Do' list of some sort.
- Consider 'making appointments' with your tasks, and / or indicating time slots where you are available to deal with colleagues

What did you really do today? – A Fresh Look at Time Management

LOCK IT IN

You should now stop reading for today. Review the definitions of 'urgency' and 'importance', and check that you understand and have considered some of your type A, B1, B2 and C tasks.

What activities do you become 'dragged into' and when do you have plenty of notice to schedule tasks in? Do you balance the types of tasks that you undertake, and how effective are the time planning aids that you currently use? A sample daily time planning aid is shown on the following page.

What did you really do today? – A Fresh Look at Time Management

Daily planner

Tuesday 30 September 2014		
REMEMBER	**APPOINTMENTS**	**NOTES**
	08.45	
	09.00	
	09.15	
	09.30	
	09.45	
	10.00	
	10.15	
	10.30	
	10.45	
PRIORITISED TASKS (A, B, C)	11.00	
	11.15	
	11.30	
	11.45	
	12.00	
	12.15	
	12.30	
	12.45	
	13.00	
	13.15	
	13.30	
	13.45	
	14.00	
	14.15	
	14.30	
	14.45	
PEOPLE TO CALL	15.00	
	15.15	
	15.30	
	15.45	
	16.00	
	16.15	
EXPENSES	16.30	
	16.45	
	17.00	

©2014 Pete Kennard

What did you really do today? – A Fresh Look at Time Management

Filing systems

Any effective person needs to be organised, and in addition to knowing what needs to be done and when, there also needs to be somewhere to put new, on-going and completed work, and this requires an appropriate filing system.

It is the *suitability* of such a filing system that can have a huge impact on one's time management, and so many people seem to struggle to get this right. And 'right' in this context means fit for purpose given the job and its core / primary responsibilities.

Estate Agents have pretty much got filing right. Go to almost any estate agents office in the country and they will probably organise paper copies of their property sales particulars in much the same way; in ascending price order with a colour code for the property type (e.g. blue for flats, red for bungalows, yellow for houses etc.) and a number denoting the number of bedrooms. The reason for this is that most people who enquire ask for "all the … with … bedrooms between £ … and £ …" and thus the system works and anyone can use it easily. And that's exactly what a good filing system should be – simple, appropriate and easy to use!

But some people get it very wrong! I recall visiting an inbound Call Centre some years ago where hard and electronic copies of client particulars were filed in account number order. The first question every caller was asked was their account number, and around 50% of people had to go away and find it leaving the operative hanging on at the end of the line for a minute or so until the customer located it. When I asked why they weren't filed by name, or address, or postcode (or in fact anything that the customer would have *known* straight away) the reply was "We've always done it that way"!

Some research suggests that 60% to 80% of what organisations file away is never referred to in that format again. If this is true then it means that a huge amount of time may be being spent

What did you really do today? – A Fresh Look at Time Management

carefully putting things away in, for example, strict alphabetical order, for no good reason. Now at the risk of introducing an oxymoron, this could mean that in some cases there is a strong argument for what I call 'rough filing'.

The term 'rough filing' refers to a form of quick filing whereby instead of putting files away in strict alphabetical order all of the A's are grouped together, and all of the B's together and so on. The result is a sort of order, but one that is much quicker to execute. And the good news is that even if you do subsequently need one of those files it can be found relatively quickly as you are only looking through $1/26^{th}$ of the lot. The result is that it is very much quicker to file things away, and only slightly slower to re-locate them. Now of course 'rough filing' is only appropriate where in most cases the file won't be needed again, but like many time management tips, in the scheme of things it has a place.

Incidentally, there is a strong argument for using this technique for any work that is pending / awaiting action / awaiting a call back. Rather than having a pile of unsorted stuff on your desk or in a tray, keeping it in rough alphabetical order makes it quicker to locate when you need it (and it's very quick to do).

The trend towards 'hot-desking', 'open-plan' offices, and 'modern-working' in general means that many of us can be less territorial about our workspaces than might previously have been the case. Notwithstanding the content of the next section, some of us (me included) have chosen to adopt a sort of 'portable' filing system that can come with us wherever we go.

My personal choice when away from the office, which in my case is frequently, is to keep three concertina-files that between them help me organise my life.

The first is a simple A to Z file where I keep (roughly sorted) the details of anybody who is essentially 'pending'. This includes, for example, those from whom I am awaiting a response, people that I am expecting to hear from before I am back in the office permanently, and details pertaining to projects that are in limbo, etc.

The next is a simple 1 to 31 file where I put things that I need to do on certain days. Thus I put everything in the slot for the 8th that I want (or need) to work on, or that I expect to do on that day. So first thing every morning, without fail, I visit my 1 to 31 file, and there is everything that requires action. I even use it for reminders, though I guess I could have written them in my diary or put them into my electronic organiser. And hey, if the 8th is a Saturday then I either take them out on the 7th or the 10th. Simple and very easy isn't it?

So let's say on the 8th I am to call Joe Bloggs, and I call him. If he agrees to get back to me on the 12th then I slip his details into that slot, or if I don't know when he's likely to 'phone back for whatever reason, I pop his file into the A to Z under 'B' (or maybe 'J' if he's a mate)!

The third of my concertina-files is much the same as a 1 to 31 except that it's a January to December. Sometimes I speak with somebody in June and they might say "call me back in September". No specific date has been agreed and they aren't likely to call me in the meantime, but I don't want to miss it so I'll slip it into my expanding file in the September slot. When September comes, or if I'm really organised at the end of August, I'll extract everything for the coming month and drop it into my 1 to 31 to deal with as I now see fit.

And that's it ... that's my portable filing system and has been for years. And it works and has served me very well indeed. Of course in my permanent office I have traditional filing cabinets and I also have boxes of archived files (it is important that every so often files that are no longer 'live' are separated from those where there could be some activity in the future), but I keep the relevant day-to-day paperwork separate from the redundant stuff that simply threatens to 'clog the system'.

What did you really do today? – A Fresh Look at Time Management

Lastly, look around for other un-necessary clutter. Here I am reminded of a visit to a Solicitors office once where there were literally rows of professional yearbooks in date order on the shelves. Clearly each 'new' one superseded the last, so in fact all but the latest were, by definition, out of date. Maybe the number of volumes was there to 'say to people' "Look how long we've been established" but I interpreted the message as "Look how long it's been since we've had a good sort out in here"!

So, take a moment to review how you and your organisation file things and ask *why* it is done that way. If the system has remained unchanged for years then perhaps the information is accessible in other formats now, meaning that the methods of filing might be able to be altered accordingly. Let's face it, filing isn't much fun, and if we could spend less of our time doing it and there was little if any negative impact on the business I think most people would welcome that outcome.

TOP TIPS

- Ensure that your filing system works for you! If it is not fit for purpose then change it!
- Are you keeping too much? How much of what you retain is ever referred to again? If the answer is "not much" then consider not keeping it, or perhaps filing it in another format.
- Are you duplicating information and storing it twice (for example, printing off e-mails un-necessarily)? Don't!
- When did you last review your filing and storage systems? Might there be a better way of doing it?

©2014 Pete Kennard

LOCK IT IN

- You should now stop reading and not continue any further until you have reviewed your filing system and made any changes that you now feel are appropriate

What did you really do today? – A Fresh Look at Time Management

Your working environment

This book isn't just for office-based workers – it is for everybody. We all have an environment in which to work, it's just that for some that environment might be a nice warm building whereas for others it could be a field or a truck!

But the environment in which you work is very important to time management since it could be either conducive to being effective or it could be a barrier to getting things done.

Many people consider that they have little if any control over this particular area of their working lives, but in fact even in the most restricted of environments there are likely to be positive adaptations that could be made.

Problems in this area might include, for example:

- Location of the workplace / space
- The actual amount of space available to you personally
- Noise / distractions (internal and external)
- Proximity to others, and in particular to disruptive individuals
- Location in relation to specific equipment, enquiries, corridors, entrances etc.
- Lighting (type and brightness etc.)
- Temperature
- Ventilation
- Tools / equipment for the job (including availability, fitness for purpose, state of repair, latest version etc.)
- Budget available for any alteration(s)
- Other limitations (e.g. listed building status etc.)

What did you really do today? – A Fresh Look at Time Management

Make a list below of all of the environmental issues that you feel could negatively impact on your personal effectiveness at work.

The default tends to be that we put up with what we're provided with at work, but if you are employed then it is likely that your employer is going to want value for money from you, and accordingly most are willing to listen to well-reasoned requests (especially where there is a fully-costed tangible benefit).

For example, it may cost thousands of pounds to upgrade a computer system, but were it to transpire that a number of staff could be more productive as a consequence, then the payback might be quite quick and thus the investment very worthwhile. Furthermore it could have knock-on effects in terms of staff morale, reduced stress and customer service, all of which well-run businesses would recognise as positive.

Likewise there would obviously be a significant expense attached to replacing old lighting in an office, but if it were proven that workers experienced fewer stress headaches (and perhaps the running costs were also reduced) might the initiative be considered?

What did you really do today? – A Fresh Look at Time Management

There is already plenty of evidence to suggest that the 'cost' of installing water coolers in some locations is recognised as negligible, especially when you consider that it is known that dehydration negatively impacts on concentration levels.

Similarly, study after study has concluded that certain colours can affect workers' moods, and in many places there has been a noticeable shift away from traditional institutional colour schemes for just this reason.

Regarding 'tools for the job' there is often a very strong argument for not simply buying cheap. For example, it is a well-known fact that some less expensive brush-cutters / strimmers have vibration rates that prevent them from being used for more than a certain length of time. However, spend just a few more pounds per unit and a similar machine might be able to be used all day.

Might installing just one extra PC in a building mean that people weren't kept hanging around waiting until it was free to use, or would fixing that broken printer sooner rather than later stop staff from having to leave their workspace and interrupt others elsewhere in the building in the meantime?

And perhaps that extra few quid for those new overalls would mean that the staff member didn't get so wet in inclement weather, and that perhaps he / she had a lower rate of sickness absence as a result.

Most initiatives that relate to the working environment *should originate* from the people actually doing the work, as it is only these individuals that <u>really</u> know what is required. So why not have a think about what would go on your 'wish list'? If you don't ask then you'll maybe never get it!

What did you really do today? – A Fresh Look at Time Management

Complete the matrix below being as specific as you can about the benefits and costs that might be incurred.

Suggestion / idea	Benefit(s)	Likely cost
For example: *Install phones with speakers or audio-conference system* Add your ideas below:	*Save multiple calls to staff about the same topic. Ability to participate in some Head Office meetings without the need to travel*	*Speaker phones approx. £30 per unit, or A/C system £250 all in*

What did you really do today? – A Fresh Look at Time Management

Okay, so that takes care of the more radical stuff, but what simple changes could you make to your workplace?

Might you be able to relocate yourself so you are not quite as close to a noisy colleague in an open-plan office? Could you maybe angle your desk away from the door or the photocopier so that you aren't in line-of-sight with everybody that comes in or uses it? Perhaps you could remove the visitors chair from close to your desk to deter people from sitting down (most people will spend longer talking when seated than when standing).

Why not take away personal items or put them out of view? Personal items are often talking points (family photographs, postcards etc.) and can be significant timewasters if the casual visitor has little to do!

If you can do so then maybe consider closing the door when you are working on something that is important (though don't keep it constantly closed as others won't recognise the significance), or make use of the 'quiet space' if your organisation is forward-thinking enough to have one.

All of the suggestions on this page cost nothing to implement and could have noticeable results in terms of effective time management. They are just examples and of course may not be suitable for you, so think about your own workspace and come up with a few of your own.

TOP TIPS

- Take a close look at your workplace, wherever or whatever it may be.
- In terms of any 'wish list', think in terms of the 'payback'. Consider any ideas in the style of a cost vs. benefit analysis.

LOCK IT IN

You should now stop reading for today. Conduct an 'audit' of your work space and make a list of everything that could be altered to improve your time management (and maybe also the effectiveness of others). Make the changes that you can personally, straight away, and submit your costed suggestions to your Manager or employer before you move on to the next section.

What did you really do today? – A Fresh Look at Time Management

Managing interruptions

Firstly let's be clear here – people will interrupt you and mess up your plans! You will no doubt have discovered this when you completed your time log, though I suspect that the only revelation may have been just how often it happens. Since this is pretty much certain then the best we can hope to do is take steps to manage these interruptions and to minimise their effect on us.

In my experience these individuals fall into two categories. The first group are those who didn't realise you were busy and 'up to your eyes' in it, and the second group are those who don't care!

Naturally the first group are the easier ones to deal with, and that is essentially down to us. Probably we haven't made it obvious enough that we're busy and that we would really prefer not to be disturbed. Perhaps we are too accommodating or welcoming or just find it difficult to say "no"?

Most reasonable people don't mind if they can't talk to us right away as long as they know when they *can* talk to us. Indeed we can even become too much of a 'rock' for others to the extent that they stop thinking for themselves! I wonder whether you have ever experienced the situation where somebody has telephoned or e-mailed something to you but for some reason or another you don't respond immediately. Maybe by the time you do get back to them they've sorted it out for themselves? In this case they probably didn't really need to contact you in the first place did they?

One method of managing interruptions involves good diary management. It is obviously important to be accessible to others but not to be too accessible as this can result in people (perhaps unwittingly) taking advantage.

What did you really do today? – A Fresh Look at Time Management

So consider making your diary accessible to others too but <u>only</u> after you have already made appointments with your tasks and blocked out corresponding chunks where you are unavailable. Do ensure that you leave some gaps or indicate when you can take calls / receive visitors, and you'll probably find that slowly but surely people will become aware of this and more of them will begin to contact you when you want them to! Think about it ... if your favourite coffee shop suddenly decides to close early on a Wednesday it may initially be irritating but you will soon adapt your habits to visit it when it is open, and perhaps to go elsewhere when it isn't available. See the parallel?

For those people who didn't realise you were busy it's all about 'education', and if you take steps to let them know they'll mostly respect your right to some uninterrupted time. In some situations it may be necessary to say something after the event, but keep it friendly and positive and things will usually improve.

For those who are less respectful the key lies in being proactive (i.e. seeking to anticipate situations where you are vulnerable to being interrupted) and behaving assertively (i.e. dealing with it honestly and directly, and considering the rights of others whilst expecting them to consider yours).

What did you really do today? – A Fresh Look at Time Management

I remember somebody on a course of mine once telling me how she was being bombarded with work-related e-mails from her Manager late into the evening on a regular basis. Whilst there was no contractual obligation for her to respond, it was felt that there was an implied expectation that she (and others who had a similar role) should do so 'for the good of the business.' Clearly this was affecting her work-life balance so she took it upon herself to set her e-mail preferences so that it sent an out-of-hours automated response along the lines of 'Thank you for your message. My hours of work are 9.00am to 5.00pm Monday to Friday and I will reply to you at the earliest opportunity upon my return to work'. Although initially fearful of her Manager's reaction to this she actually received an apology from him and evidently he too took time to reconsider his own work-life balance as well.

Initially confronting those who might otherwise take advantage may seem daunting, but the pay-off is often well worth it and very empowering!

Perhaps others regularly seem to 'dump' work on you? Note that there is a difference between being delegated to and dumped on, and this deals only with the latter.

An assertive person might respond to someone attempting to dump work on them along the lines of "I can do this for you, but if I do then I won't be able to do ... until ... Just checking that you're happy with that?", or "I'm too busy at the moment (doing ...). Have you asked ...?"

If somebody approaches you at an inconvenient time then you might want to start the conversation with "I only have five minutes right now. Is that enough or would you prefer to speak with me later, say at 2.30pm?" or even "I have no time at the moment, but I can speak with you at 2.30pm".

What did you really do today? – A Fresh Look at Time Management

It is said that a picture speaks a thousand words and very often non-verbal communication (a.k.a. body language) can be used to good effect to reinforce key messages. For example, standing up when somebody approaches you (and remaining standing) can communicate that you wish the meeting to be brief. Likewise checking one's watch (whilst maybe not very subtle) can also convey that time is limited!

Consider some of the situations where you could be interrupted, together with some strategies as to how to deal with them by completing the matrix below.

Nature of interruption	Was it intentional Y/N	Possible response

What did you really do today? – A Fresh Look at Time Management

Assertiveness and time management

This book is not really about assertiveness, though it should be said that in order to be effective, one needs to behave assertively. And assertiveness can be defined in a number of ways, though few would argue with "Standing up for your rights without violating the rights of other people" as a generic definition.

The reasons why there are important links between the subjects of effective time management and assertion are that the most common alternative options, namely passive or aggressive behaviour are clearly ineffective. The former allows for individuals to be taken advantage of largely because of their failure to protect themselves, whilst the latter often results in bullying tactics with the aggressor's own agenda being the only one that is considered.

Assertive people are honest and direct (without being offensive). They tend to focus on issues rather than personalities, solutions rather than problems, and don't look to apportion blame.

Sometimes rather than go head-to-head and challenge others' views directly, they may choose to do so by asking appropriate questions. For example, rather than saying "that's a load of complete rubbish", they might instead ask "and how did you arrive at that conclusion?"

Characteristically they will use plenty of ownership within their dialogue, for example using the word 'I' on a regular basis such as "I understand", "I need / want", "as I see it", and "from my point of view" etc.

It is recommended that you read upon and /or attend some training on the subject, though in the meantime it might be helpful to consider how you might respond in some of the following situations. Please consider the prompts, and respond using an assertive statement or question.

What did you really do today? – A Fresh Look at Time Management

1. "I need that report on my desk in ten minutes" (assume that the requester is your Manager and that you have lots of other work to do)

....

2. "I just need a quick word with you – it won't take a moment" (assume that the speaker is a colleague and has just 'barged in')

....

3. "If you could just sort that for me before you do the work for Barry. I don't suppose he'll mind" (assume Barry is your Manager and the requester isn't)

....

4. "The paper is stuck in the copier. I told Jan that you'd fix it for her. She's waiting for you now" (assume that the speaker and Jan are two colleagues and that there are plenty of other people with the necessary knowhow in the office)

....

5. "I can see you're busy so I'll just sit here and wait" (assume the speaker has just dropped by without warning and that you're busy)

....

What did you really do today? – A Fresh Look at Time Management

Before you move on, satisfy yourself that the responses you have come up with are appropriate and that, given that specific situation, you would be comfortable saying them.

If you are in any doubt it may help to revisit the sentence that you wrote previously about your position that contained your job title, the main responsibilities, and outcome(s) of your role.

TOP TIPS

- Interruptions cannot be prevented altogether. The best that you can (realistically) hope for is to manage them.
- Those who interrupt you will fall into one of two categories; those who don't realise the effects of their actions, and those who don't care!
- Make sure that people know *when* they can talk to you. Some people will respect that. Why not indicate in your diary the times when you are 'available'?
- Initially confronting those who take advantage may seem daunting, but the pay-off is often worth it and very empowering.
- In order to deal effectively with those who try to take advantage, it is necessary to behave assertively. Why not consider developing your skills with some assertiveness training?

LOCK IT IN

- You should now stop reading for today. Think about the people who routinely interrupt you. Do you think their behaviour is intentional or unintentional? Also, were you comfortable responding to the prompts on the previous page, and, more importantly, would you actually say that? If not, then book yourself onto an assertiveness course immediately!

What did you really do today? – A Fresh Look at Time Management

Meetings

Without doubt one of the biggest 'time thieves' for a lot of people is meetings, with many citing these as the largest single cause of lost productivity. The regular (weekly or monthly) meeting is legendary in organisations across the land, yet so often they are run very ineffectively.

In one of my former workplaces I personally witnessed the 'Monday meeting' grow from a relatively brief update lasting about an hour with four participants to an assembly of around a dozen that lasted more than four hours and frequently extended into lunch! The tripling in the number of attendees and the huge lengthening of the duration would not, in itself, have been an issue had all of the content been relevant to all of the people for all of the time. But the bottom line was that at the end we were only covering slightly more than we had been initially with a huge increase in 'cost'.

And make no mistake about it, meetings 'cost' a great deal both in terms of time spent (factor in wages, travel, refreshments etc.) and opportunity cost (i.e. what else you and everyone else *might* have been doing instead). So, next time you have a meeting, just do this calculation. It's very rough, but it is often quite an 'eye opener'.

- Number of attendees .... (A)
- Average hourly rate in £* .... (B)
- Average number of hours invested** .... (C)
- Cost of venue in £*** .... (D)
- Cost of travel in £**** .... (E)
- Other costs in £***** .... (F)

What did you really do today? – A Fresh Look at Time Management

* Generally it is accepted that 'on costs' (National Insurance contributions, pension provision, sickness and holiday absence costs, training, etc.) average around 50% of one's hourly rate, so don't forget to multiply hourly rates by 1.5 in your calculations to get a more representative figure.

** In calculating the average number of hours invested, remember to include preparatory time (e.g. reading the agenda, preparing reports etc.) and travel time both to and from the meeting. Also, don't overlook post-meeting time which may involve looking over the minutes or undertaking activities which were agreed as your responsibility.

*** In estimating the cost of the venue, include room hire rates (where applicable) and any refreshments. Where these are prepared 'freely' by colleagues, factor in their 'lost' time too! Also, there may be a requirement for equipment which may need to be hired.

**** In terms of travel expenses, calculate fuel / expenses payments, parking, tolls, taxi fares and overnight accommodation where applicable. In certain cases wear and tear may need to be included.

***** Other costs can be significant. These might include the obvious tangible things such as photocopying, equipment hire, advertising or signage, or extend to the less obvious such as 'cover' at work for those who are away as a consequence of the meeting taking place. Questions that might be worth considering include "What else might I have been doing instead of this?", "Is other work going to be delayed (or delegated) as a result of my being here?", and even "What extra pressures / stress am I going to experience because of the meeting?"

Not including the intangibles, the cost in £'s approximates to (AxBxC)+D+E+F. How much did your last meeting (or how much might your next one) cost?

£ ....

You will no doubt have a view as to whether it was 'worth it'!

What did you really do today? – A Fresh Look at Time Management

You could be forgiven for thinking that I am quite anti-meeting but nothing could be further from the truth. My belief is that meetings play an important part in any progressive organisation's day-to-day operation and that they are crucial for its development. But to maximise their effectiveness I believe there are certain, let's call them 'rules of good practice', that must be adhered to. For the purposes of this publication I have set them out in the form of a checklist below, with questions attached to some. When considering these, the answer "because we've always done it that way" is not an acceptable one!

1. Agenda: Every meeting *must* have an agenda and this should be circulated prior to the event taking place to allow participants to prepare adequately. Springing things on people is rarely an effective approach as it both lengthens proceedings and can result in ill-thought-through and sometimes wholly inappropriate discussions taking place.

2. Participants: The number of attendees should be kept to an absolute minimum. Only those who actually need to attend should do so, and those who have an interest in only a part of the meeting (perhaps to report or be consulted on something within their remit) should attend just those parts that are relevant to them, preferably towards the beginning.

3. Records: Minutes should always be taken. Depending upon the nature of the meeting it may be that these are taken by a secretary or by one of the participants.

    In the case of the latter it could be that these are fairly brief and in the form of bullet points, but unless there is some record of proceedings then people's 'selective memories' may distort their recollection of what actually took place.

    Furthermore, if action points aren't recorded then these can be left uncompleted, and every action should be attributed to an individual at the meeting who then has responsibility for seeing that it progresses. Finally with regard to the minutes, they should be written-up and circulated to all attendees at the earliest opportunity and in every case well before the next meeting (at which point they should be signed-off).

What did you really do today? – A Fresh Look at Time Management

4. Times: It is good practice to indicate both a start and finish time as this helps to focus peoples' minds. Where no finish time is given, meetings very often last until the person with the most to say or least to do has had enough, and that could be long after you! Where possible, it may even be prudent to attach indicative timings for each agenda item as this can help the Chair keep proceedings moving.

5. Chair: Every meeting should have a Chair(person). He / she is responsible for ensuring that the meeting runs to time and that protocols and best practice are both shared and followed. The Chair should not aim to influence voting, although he / she may have a vote on some issues. In every case the Chair should make it clear where he / she has an interest (i.e. a particular closeness) to a particular agenda item.

6. AOB: There should <u>not</u> be a final agenda item of 'any other business' (AOB). This is one of the biggest time-wasters of all since it allows anybody to raise anything, and is often known to take as long as the rest of the other agenda items put together. AOB is an 'invitation' for people to 'shoot from the hip', introducing random issues that (by definition) other attendees have no idea are coming. As a consequence it can result in protracted, subjective, inappropriate and maybe even inaccurate dialogue. It also devalues the purpose of the meeting because it encourages individuals not to submit items for the agenda in advance. Instead of AOB, why not have 'items for the next meeting' instead? This way the subject can be tabled, and others can prepare beforehand. And should something arise between meetings, the person could just contact the Chair and request that it be added to the agenda so that others are forewarned.

7. Scheduling: Regarding the frequency and timing of meetings, might it be wise to vary these slightly? For example, instead of having a meeting every Monday at 9.00am, maybe alternate between mornings and afternoons or perhaps even change the day. We've already established that people have different personal energy cycles and it would be a shame if the levels of some were regularly low before the meeting even started!

©2014 Pete Kennard

8. **Access:** In point (2) above I referred to the proposed number of participants. If any need to travel to the venue, would it be possible to allow them access to the proceedings via other media rather than attending in person? For example, many organisations have video-conferencing facilities in-house and most could audio-conference using equipment that they already have. Even where this is not currently available it can often be purchased or leased quite cheaply, with any investment very quickly potentially repaid.

9. **Location:** Are you holding your meetings in the most appropriate location? Is it convenient for everybody? Is there sufficient parking etc.? Might the location be off-putting for some (perhaps due to accessibility or maybe because it's at Head Office and going there is a bit scary?).

10. **Interruptions:** Can you ensure that there will be no interruptions? Phones (both land lines and mobiles) should be switched off. The door should be closed and others should not disturb proceedings, other than in a genuine emergency.

11. **Environment:** The Chair should ensure that the environment is conducive to getting things done. Consider the layout, the furniture, temperature, lighting and acoustics etc. Everything should be fit for purpose.

12. **Biscuits:** Refreshments (or at least refreshment breaks) should be considered if and where they aid concentration. However, meetings are about work and not about freebies, and coming along just because you get nice biscuits is not in itself a justification for having them!

13. **Training:** It may be appropriate to think about arranging training for the Chair and / or Minute Taker as these are pivotal roles. Well run and well documented meetings should be the aim, and anything that facilitates this should be considered.

14. **Consult:** Why not *ask* the people that usually come to your meetings what they think? In my experience the best ideas for positive change often come from those most directly involved.

What did you really do today? – A Fresh Look at Time Management

How many of the above 'rules' have you or your organisation already adopted?

Are there any suggestions that you would like to adopt? (Note how popular they may be with others, and where and why there could be any 'barriers').

Do you have any ideas / suggestions that are not captured above?

What did you really do today? – A Fresh Look at Time Management

TOP TIPS

- Avoid impromptu meetings. These are very disruptive and huge 'time thieves'. Create a culture where all meetings must have a 24 hour lead time as a minimum.
- Only hold a meeting where there is a purpose, and question the true value of the 'regular' meeting
- Every meeting should have an agenda. If one is not provided, *ask* for it. How can you be expected to make a meaningful contribution if topics are 'sprung' on you unexpectedly?
- Start (and finish) on time. Don't wait for late-comers, and consider allowing a specific amount of time for each agenda item.
- Abolish AOB (Any Other Business). Instead, replace it with 'items for next time'.

LOCK IT IN

Unless you never attend meetings you should now stop reading for today. Reflect on how much time you typically spend at meetings and the 'value' you truly get from them. In many organisations meetings seem steeped in tradition, and unless this culture is challenged, they will continue to waste huge amounts of time long into the future.

Delegation

If you were thinking of not reading this section on the basis that "I have nobody to delegate anything to" then put that thought to one side. Within this section we will naturally look at what is traditionally considered delegation, but also at delegating 'upwards' and simply asking for help.

It probably comes as no surprise that the starting point for what to delegate is the prioritising grid that we looked at on page 32. Where tasks are *your* responsibility and where they should (or can) only be done by you, then these cannot be delegated. Those that should be considered as opportunities are the ones that could be done by another person, and that in terms of importance are towards the left hand side of the matrix as it is shown in this publication. The most obvious choices are the B2 group (though type C activities may also be candidates for being completed by somebody else).

Delegation could be defined as 'organised sharing of responsibility', and it is wise to remember this. Accountability is at the very heart of delegation, and where an individual is required to do something, then they should always be recognised for their contribution. With this in mind, the delegator (i.e. you) should think about their experience, knowledge and skills, since getting the mix of attributes right is important to ensure that the job gets done. It is also key to think about their current workload (helping to reduce it if necessary), as if they are already swamped with work then it is unlikely that they will be of much assistance to you!

The brief about exactly what is required is a crucial component of the process too. Remember that what is being delegated will make complete sense to you but that, by definition, it will be new to the other party. Thus correctly and effectively communicating the details is of paramount importance. A good way to do this is to get the delegate to confirm the requirements back to you.

What did you really do today? – A Fresh Look at Time Management

'Letting go' can be a problem for many, and the balance between providing support and interference is another significant one. Delegates who are undertaking unfamiliar work need to be carefully selected and clearly briefed to give them the best chance of success, but also need to know how to obtain assistance if necessary. But most will not welcome having somebody 'checking up' on them or 'looking over their shoulder' all the time, and again it is often prudent to ask them to report to you at specific times as this helps promote ownership and responsibility. Furthermore if they don't comply, it gives the delegator a reason to 'check in'.

In addition to helping with your workload, delegation affords the opportunity to develop the skills of other people, benefitting both individuals and the organisation alike. This means that providing balanced positive feedback is also important, as is saying "thank you" for helping out. But take care not to always delegate to the same person; whilst they might be willing, it is potentially unfair on others not to spread the opportunity for development.

And what if there are no 'natural' candidates to delegate to? Well, what about asking your boss? If this appeals to you then I would suggest that you aim to 'sell' the idea to them, that is to say highlight the benefits (e.g. "If you could help out with ... then I'll be able to do ..." or "If you could arrange for ... then it will mean ... for the team"). Don't think in terms of WIIFM (What's In It For Me) but instead WIIFY (What's In It For You).

Asking for help is not technically the same as delegation, though it is included in this section as there are parallels in terms of both when it may be necessary and how it might be done. It is most likely that this option will be used for A and B1 activities, though since these are really *your* responsibility, it will normally be assistance that is asked for rather than transfer of ownership. Sometimes there are smaller parts or sub-tasks that can be delegated in their entirety, but not the whole thing. When asking for help, think of the 'pay off' for the person who is supporting you.

What did you really do today? – A Fresh Look at Time Management

A checklist for delegating:

- Is the task or activity suitable for delegation?
- Is the delegate both willing and able? (In terms of 'able', consider their workload as well as their attributes)
- Is the brief clear and unambiguous?
- Has the delegate confirmed their understanding?
- What support might be necessary to ensure success? (Can you provide this?)
- Are you truly able to 'let go'? (Be honest – some people find this difficult)
- Are you satisfied that you have you delegated ownership, responsibility and accountability?
- Do you have appropriate reporting procedures in place?
- If you delegate regularly, do you spread the opportunity (rather than select the same individual(s) every time)?

Make a note below of tasks or activities that you might be able to delegate.

Note any barriers to delegation that you might encounter.

Motivation

Motivation is essentially the will to act, and it is acknowledged that there is a link between levels of motivation and productivity / performance in the workplace.

Theorist Abraham Maslow identified five areas of need, believing that satisfying the most basic (i.e. 'physiological' and 'safety' needs) is not enough to motivate people sufficiently. 'Social', 'esteem' and 'self-actualization' are all steps on the ladder towards many people's aspirations, with the majority seeking elements of at least some of these to enthuse them.

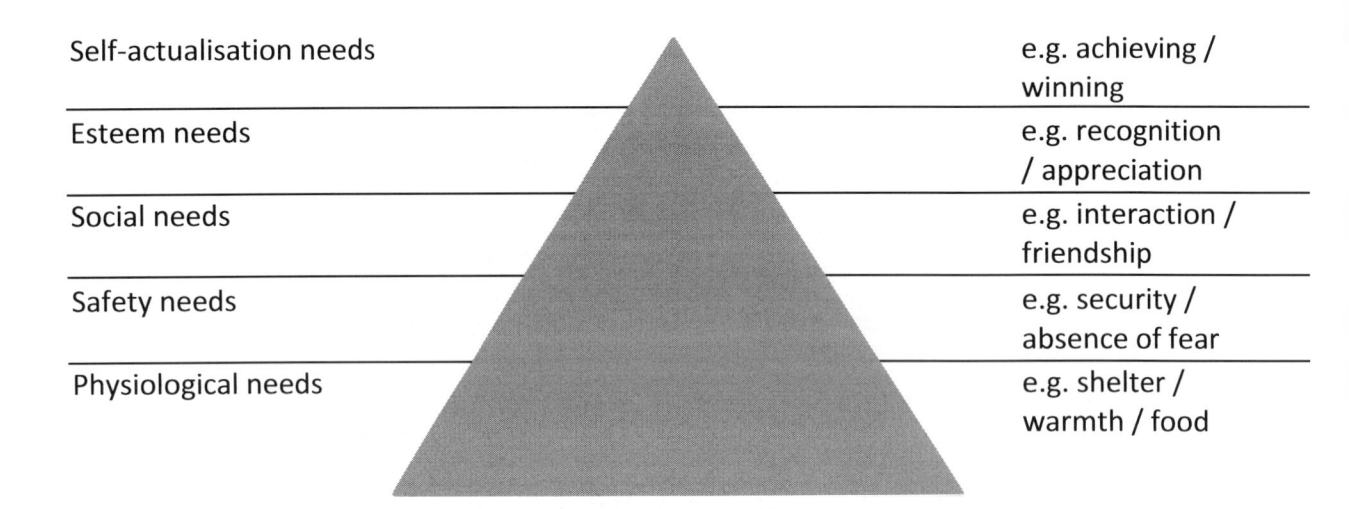

Self-actualisation needs	e.g. achieving / winning
Esteem needs	e.g. recognition / appreciation
Social needs	e.g. interaction / friendship
Safety needs	e.g. security / absence of fear
Physiological needs	e.g. shelter / warmth / food

Psychologist Frederick Herzberg also developed a theory for motivation, though his was based on 'hygiene factors' (a set of basic human workplace needs) and 'motivators' (what drives people towards success).

Countless studies have been completed with many recognising the value of happiness at work and how it seems to result in improved outcomes. And given that this may not appear to most

What did you really do today? – A Fresh Look at Time Management

to be 'rocket science' it is all the more surprising that some organisations seem not to focus much attention on it.

When asked what would raise their motivation, most staff members would probably reply "more money", but fiscal remuneration has only a short-term motivational effect. Longer-lasting job enrichment may come from a number of factors such as providing variety in the work, a supportive environment, involvement in decision-making, recognising achievements and so on, with the definitive list being a very personal thing. Think about what motivates you to go to work, and specifically what motivates you to do what you currently do. If you can't think of anything other than the money, then it is possible that your potential may be restricted.

So there are two aspects for the good time manager here. Firstly, what can you do to motivate yourself? And secondly, what can be done to motivate those around you (and in particular those whose efforts impact upon your personal effectiveness)?

Think of motivation as being the 'turbo' for your engine. If you can deploy it at the right times, performance can be improved considerably!

Note below some aspects of life that enthuse you or that you enjoy?

What did you really do today? – A Fresh Look at Time Management

How many of these are available to you at work?

✏️

Has your level of motivation at work altered over time?

✏️

If so, how (and why) has it changed?

✏️

What did you really do today? – A Fresh Look at Time Management

Another area of motivation is linked to procrastination (i.e. putting things off). Some people procrastinate because they are simply disorganised, whilst others may be dissuaded from undertaking tasks or activities because they don't find them particularly appealing.

I am reminded of a conversation I had with my manager many years ago where we were discussing why staff members may not complete something that has been asked of them (and sometimes that they had agreed to do).

His view was that there are really just three underlying reasons why people won't finish (or in certain cases even start) a job. These are:

1. They didn't fully understand the brief or don't know how to do it, or
2. Somebody or something delayed or prevented them from doing it, or
3. They don't really want to do it

On the face of it this didn't appear to be an earth-shattering revelation, but on closer consideration the third reason *is* one that most of us recognise but that few will admit to, especially when at work (and in particular to their boss)! Furthermore when we aren't really keen to do something we often try to 'justify' not doing it (to ourselves or to others) by making excuses, probably citing a problem that stopped us. So the next time you or a colleague miss a deadline and explain it away by saying "I would have completed it but …", ask yourself whether that is the real reason or whether it is a 'smokescreen'.

What did you really do today? – A Fresh Look at Time Management

TOP TIPS

- Most people have the scope to delegate certain tasks, and in the main these should be those that are category B2 or C on your prioritising grid.
- When delegating, don't present that rationale as WIIFM ('What's In It For Me') but rather WIIFY ('What's In It For You'), as there should be some benefit for the delegate.
- Before you delegate something, refer to the checklist (on page 69).
- Somebody once said "It's your attitude rather than aptitude that determine your altitude". Likewise, the saying "Those that want to might, whilst those that don't, won't" rings quite true!
- Countless studies have concluded that people that are happy at work are more productive overall than those who are not. Think about what motivates you, and consider to what extent these factors are present in the workplace.

LOCK IT IN

- You should now stop reading for today. Reflect on your opportunities for delegation, and consider what motivates you and those around you. Think about the extent to which levels of enthusiasm for work can impact on your time management.

What did you really do today? – A Fresh Look at Time Management

Deal with things only once!

One of the golden principles of good time management is to aim to deal with things only once. Now of course in some cases this won't be possible, but this principle should always be one's goal.

Prior to being introduced to this concept, my workspace was always something of a mess. When challenged I always claimed to know where everything was (in some cases even using 'creativity' as my justification), but the truth was that I was just dis-organised. I had various piles of paperwork; 'in trays', an 'out tray' and several 'pending trays' and it was this last tray that was the biggest problem.

Like so many things to do with being effective the solution is really quite a simple one. And basically, it works like this. Every time you receive something, be that a piece of paper, a message, or even an e-mail, aim to make one of five decisions on how to proceed with it. (In some cases the same choices can even apply to decision-making). Your options are:

- Deal with it (i.e. do it now before you do anything else)
- Delegate it (i.e. give it away)
- Schedule it (i.e. plan a time to do it)
- File it, or
- Bin it!

Naturally the choice(s) you make will be determined by a number of factors, not least what your role is, where *it* originated from, and how much notice you have been given, but notwithstanding these points the principles are pretty much the same.

What did you really do today? – A Fresh Look at Time Management

There is generally merit in **dealing with it** when either it is a genuine priority A task and time is very short, or where to do anything else will take as long (or longer) than actually completing it straight away.

The choice to **delegate it** is natural where it is a B2 task and you have a deputy, but in other cases this may mean simply asking for some assistance from a colleague (or even your manager). Remember to think about 'chunking' tasks (i.e. breaking them down into smaller pieces) as this may create opportunities for passing on a part of an activity where to get rid of the lot would not be an option.

Normally it is appropriate to **schedule in** activities where you are given a reasonably lengthy lead-time. But take care to only schedule those that really are your responsibility (B1 tasks) and not those that might have come your way inappropriately!

File it when that is where it belongs! If it shouldn't be on your desk (or in your e-mail 'in box') then ensure that it resides where it can be easily found when necessary. Sometimes when you are waiting for a response to something but you can't be sure when that is going to be, to have some sort of order to things in the interim can be a real bonus.

How much are you keeping 'just in case'? The decision to **bin it** may be a bold one, but most of us are not ruthless enough when it comes to throwing things away. Far too many people have stuff quite literally gathering dust that will never be needed, and again have e-mail 'in boxes' overflowing with messages that could be deleted. Assuming that there isn't some law or procedure that requires you to retain it, think seriously about doing some 'Spring cleaning'!

What did you really do today? – A Fresh Look at Time Management

Here are some questions for you.

- Do you have a pending file? (If so, give some serious thought to getting rid of it)
- Do you have information in duplicate? (E.g. do you routinely print your e-mails?)
- Do you take on too much work or feel awkward / reluctant to ask others for help? (You may wish to think about some assertiveness training)
- When was the last time you went through your work and actually looked for things to throw away / delete? (Do it first thing tomorrow)

Put another way, is there anything that you are currently doing that might stop you from applying the 'deal, delegate, schedule, file, bin' principle?

TOP TIPS

- Be ruthless! Avoid duplicating things and aim to deal with it, delegate it, schedule it, file it, or bin it (on receipt).
- If you have one, get rid of your 'pending' tray.

LOCK IT IN

- You should now stop reading for today. This section is deliberately quite short as for many people it requires a re-think as to how they approach their tasks. Before you move on to the next part of this workbook, spend a day or two applying the principle to everything that you encounter.

What did you really do today? – A Fresh Look at Time Management

Reading

Ever stopped to wonder how much time you spend reading 'stuff' at work each week? I'll bet if you added it all up it would equate to a fair chunk of your time.

But the big question is just how relevant the material which you read actually is to the *key* elements of your role, and the big problem is that in most cases you don't know until you've read it (and by then valuable time has been expended already)!

Considerations when reading include:

- Does it have to be read *now* or could it be kept 'til later?
- Does it *need* to be read at all?
- Do you have to read the whole thing, or could the key elements be summarised in some way?
- Could somebody else read it and let you know the salient points?
- Could it be 'binned' altogether
- Should you have ever received it in the first place? (I.e. are you on a circulation list that you shouldn't or needn't be on?)

Unfortunately it seems that many people subscribe to the 'knowledge is power' school of thinking, reasoning that they'd better check everything out *just in case* it contains that golden nugget of information. So the starting point has to be to re-visit the content (or context) of the text against the sentence / paragraph that you wrote previously that describes your role. Where the material is truly relevant, read it, but where it is not then don't.

If it doesn't have to be read straight away, consider keeping it for later. Many effective time managers maintain a file of documents / information for reading when they have a few minutes

What did you really do today? – A Fresh Look at Time Management

to spare (perhaps when travelling to work by public transport, or when being kept waiting for an appointment etc.).

One of the best tips that I was ever given was to get into the habit of reading printed matter with a highlighter pen to hand, so that I could mark the key points if I needed to refer to them later. This way it is much faster the second time round and it is easier to locate specifics. If using a highlighter pen then do ensure that it is a light colour such as yellow (as darker colours come out black when photocopying), or of course use a pencil instead.

Alternatively you may wish to consider a speed reading course. For heavy readers the payback can be enormous. A good friend and colleague of mine offers one whereby after just a few hours of training it is possible to speed read an average size novel (say 200 to 300 pages) in around an hour! Imagine how those time savings could add up.

On average how much time do you spend reading at work?

Of what you read, estimate the proportion that you could have done without.

What did you really do today? – A Fresh Look at Time Management

Writing

It is said that one should 'write for the reader', the rationale being that where the recipient can't follow the content or where it is unnecessarily technical, then frankly it has been a waste of time!

Historically, organisations employed large(r) numbers of professional writers (e.g. Secretaries in typing pools etc.) though increasingly more and more of us are required to do our own writing, and in many cases typing. Now these professional writers were trained and were thus fast and accurate, but we may not have received formal tuition and as a consequence we probably achieve fewer words per minute and make considerably more mistakes!

Writing generally takes longer than talking, so ask yourself whether it is the best medium to use for the transmission of the issue(s) in question. It also says a lot about us (for example a report full of errors may cause the reader to doubt the integrity of its conclusions because it looks to have been put together carelessly). Think of it another way; would a good old-fashioned chat be more effective instead?

Remember that writing is permanent, and also that without the benefit of voice tones it can be open to interpretation, so be clear about what you want to convey. Every time somebody asks you to clarify something it means that the clarity wasn't there in the first place!

And if it *must* be written, consider the most appropriate medium. Options include letter, fax, e-mail, report, memo etc., and each has its own style and benefits / pitfalls.

There are, of course, plenty of tools to help us in our work. Grammar and spell checkers are available on most word processing packages (though it never ceases to amaze me how many people don't use them or have them on the wrong settings; having 'English – US' rather than 'English – UK' as a default is a common one).

Maybe more use could be made of standard / stock letters for common issues whereby most of the text is pre-prepared. This allows for just changing small parts of the content, usually resulting in greater speed and fewer mistakes.

How many authors of reports, I wonder, ever take the time to ask their readers how helpful or useful they found the document? Did it contain the necessary information in the right quantities? Was it reader-friendly or did it appear daunting? Was the layout appropriate?

How many circulars or staff briefings have readers who never progress beyond the second paragraph because they found it boring, irrelevant or just plain 'stuffy'? And how many times do organisations 'hide behind' a statement along the lines of "well it was on page eight of the newsletter we e-mailed you last June, so you should know about it"?

There is evidence to suggest that most people make decisions about a piece of written material very early on in their reading of it. This decision usually involves a conscious or unconscious analysis of the validity of the text, and in some cases whether or not to read on. Those in Marketing will usually say that if you don't *capture* the interest of your reader in the first sentence or two of a 'cold' communication then you'll probably lose them altogether, as consumers particularly tend to look at it with a WIIFM (what's in it for me?) mentality. Perhaps we could do worse than to think of our writing in terms of a WIIFY (what's in it for you?) way, where the 'you' is the reader(s).

What did you really do today? – A Fresh Look at Time Management

Consider the following questions.

- Who do you write for?
- How much do you know about them?
- Are you writing something that your reader(s) *need* or *want*?
- Do you (or could you) make use of templates / standard letters?
- If the text is lengthy, are there ways for readers to find what they are looking for easily? For example, is there a summary or do you make use of sub-headings, bold type, italics or bullet points?
- Does your written work ever result in questions / queries from the reader(s)? If so, it probably wasn't wholly effective first time
- Do you write in draft first and edit later? This is normally quicker than trying to do both as you go along
- Have you ever *asked* for feedback about your written work?

Effective written communication is about the accurate transmission of a message or messages from one party to another, and unlike a conversation is often a one-way process (as it may not be easy to question the writer). If your work is likely to be unread, disregarded or misunderstood then you are wasting your time!

TOP TIPS

- Be selective about what you read and when you read it.
- Aim to read things only once. Marking relevant sections with a pencil or highlighter pen can save time if you have to refer to the document later.
- Consider a speed reading course if you have to read a lot.
- Before you write something, ask yourself whether the written medium is the most appropriate. (Perhaps a 'phone call would suffice?).
- If you *must* write, ensure that you do so with the recipient(s) in mind.
- Write first and edit later. It's usually quicker.

What did you really do today? – A Fresh Look at Time Management

LOCK IT IN

You should now stop reading for today. Reflect on what you read at or for your work. Ask yourself how much you could 'live without' and take immediate action to stop what you can. Likewise consider what you write and who you write for. Have you reviewed your written work recently? If not, do it now using the bulleted prompts on the previous page.

What did you really do today? – A Fresh Look at Time Management

E-mail and mobile devices

Years ago if people wanted something and it couldn't be dealt with over the 'phone, they wrote a letter. The writer would probably allow two or three days for it to arrive at its destination, another couple of days for it to be dealt with, and a further two or three days for the reply to arrive. Then along came the fax machine and this sped up the process somewhat, with customers now expecting responses in shortened timescales. But with the advent of e-mail and mobile devices those expectations rose still further, and for many people the pressures are at an all-time-high as messages arrive at an alarming and seemingly increasing rate, with the originators demanding ever-faster action.

In terms of time management this is a growing and very significant problem for a great number of individuals as it results in too much 'fire-fighting' and everything becomes elevated to 'crisis' level. I constantly hear the cry that "e-mail is taking over" and is "blighting" peoples' lives, But e-mail will only 'take over' if we allow it to, and if we work smart and learn to 'tame' our in-boxes then it is a battle that we don't necessarily have to lose!

The strategies outlined in this section all work for some, but as is so often the case with time management initiatives, they won't all be appropriate for *you*. So read this section carefully and use your own judgement when deciding upon the ideas to adopt, but do ensure that you adopt some!

Let us start with **inbound messages**. Checking your e-mail regularly during the day can be an effective way to keep your in-box at manageable levels, but whatever you do <u>don't</u> check it too often. Constant interruptions and switching from what you were doing to check that message dramatically lower productivity and disrupt your ability to enter a state of flow when working on demanding tasks. It is not just the time it takes to open and read the message itself, it's the additional time it takes to get back to where you were, and this can often take longer than you think!

What did you really do today? – A Fresh Look at Time Management

One strategy that effective people use is to check their e-mail only at set (scheduled) points during the working day, perhaps first thing in the morning, around lunchtime, and then mid-afternoon (most messages aren't so urgent that they couldn't wait a couple of hours to be opened). Indeed, a lot of software can be set to allow you to 'receive' messages only at certain times so that you're not distracted by incoming mail (much like a postal delivery). And if you really can't do this, at least ensure that audible and visual alerts are off!

Try to schedule the checking of your e-mail to coincide with your personal energy cycle and work schedule, and perhaps let others know that you visit your in-box regularly during the day, but not 'on-demand'! Encourage others to make (sensible) use of system flags, marking messages as urgent when they really are.

When it comes to reading messages, do so intelligently. Aim to adopt the (previously referred to) principle of the *deal with it, delegate it, schedule it, file it, bin it* approach, using the first option for anything that can be completed in less than two minutes. The idea behind this is that even if it is fairly low priority, if it can be dealt with and thus got rid of that quickly then it is probably best to do so. For those that might take longer than two minutes use the most appropriate option from the remaining four. Again, some e-mail programs allow you to highlight, flag or star messages that need a response, so if yours does then consider utilising this handy feature when you can.

Every time you visit your in-box, aim to move everything out of it! Your in-box is <u>not</u> a place to keep things, so set up a simple filing system to move messages into. Call them what you like (e.g. 'Action', 'Reference', 'Waiting' etc.) and work in much the same way as you would with paper documents. The advantage of this is that it makes searching for past messages much easier. Instead of having to scour your entire e-mail system you simply search the appropriate folder. It also helps ensure that those messages requiring action aren't missed.

Certain e-mail systems allow for 'Rules' to be set up whereby messages with particular words in the subject line are automatically put into a specific folder, negating the need for you to move them manually. This can be immensely helpful, especially for non-urgent FYI (For Your Information) type messages. Why not see if your system allows or supports this?

Why not consider having certain non-essential messages re-routed to a second(ary) e-mail address if you can't use rules to have them instantly delivered to a specific folder. This could help keep your primary in-box clear, and they'll all be in a single place, ready for you to read at a suitable time.

Finally, if you regularly correspond with certain people and their messages are such that they could be shortened or perhaps be dealt with over the telephone then why not let them know? Trying to promote good e-mail strategies is not rude; on the contrary they might even thank you for it!

So, to summarise:

- Take control of your in-box (visiting it regularly but when you want to)
- Organise your e-mail and set up folders
- Utilise the 'two-minute rule' for inbound messages
- Investigate the features that your system supports
- Consider re-routing certain types of mail
- Make use of 'flags' and encourage others to do the same
- Keep other people informed, ask them to send you less, and advocate good practice / effective communication strategies at your workplace

What impression do you create with your **outbound messages**? Here are some simple rules that you can follow to ensure that your mail is received in a positive way.

What did you really do today? – A Fresh Look at Time Management

The subject line is all important. In much the same way as a newspaper headline, the subject line of an e-mail should tell the reader what the text is all about and help them decide whether or not to read on. Thus, a subject line of simply "Meeting" is of no use at all, whilst "Agenda for Planning Meeting at 10.00am on 30th September" is far more effective.

If you can put *all* of the information in the subject line, consider the EOM (End of Message) technique. Basically, putting EOM at the end of the subject line means that there is nothing further to read, and that the e-mail does not need to be opened. An example would be "Room 356 confirmed for your appraisal meeting at 3.30pm on Thursday. EOM".

It is good practice to try and make just one main point per e-mail. Therefore, if you need to write to somebody about several different issues, consider breaking the text up and sending a separate mail for each one. Far from complicating things it actually makes it *easier* for the recipient since he / she can manage their own in-box more effectively. Furthermore they can also reply to each part specifically, which may mean that you get a response to certain topics more quickly than would otherwise have been the case.

If you have to put several points into a single mail (perhaps because they relate to the same project), give consideration to presenting each point in a separate, numbered paragraph. This can make each stand out, making it far more likely that none will be missed.

Always be specific about what you want from your e-mails in terms of the recipient's response. This might be a reply, phone call or meeting etc., so be sure to include your contact details to make it easy for them to do so. Where possible, put the onus on *them* to do something.

Remember that e-mail is permanent in the same way as any other written message, and also that it is (often legally) binding. Beware of being too informal and also of using too many abbreviations. Use your spell checker and avoid slang terms or too much humour. E-mails can be printed out, and you never know where they might end up!

Use your 'Out of Office' automated response where you will be unable to check your messages. This allows the sender to consider communicating with somebody else if he / she needs a prompt reply, and also stops them bothering you again to chase you up because they didn't realise you were absent.

Similarly, where an inbound e-mail demands a detailed response (or where you need to make enquiries that may take some time to be satisfied), consider sending a 'holding' reply that advises when the originator can expect to receive something comprehensive. This practice is good customer service and again helps prevent those unwanted 'chasers'.

So again, in summary:

- Make proper use of the subject line
- Use the EOM technique where appropriate
- If possible, focus on one point per e-mail (and where you can't, number your paragraphs)
- Specify your expectations from the recipient
- Write correctly and well
- Make sensible use of automated and holding responses

In **all cases** make appropriate use of features such as urgent flags, read receipts, automated responses, digital signatures, copies (including blind copies) and disclaimers etc.

What did you really do today? – A Fresh Look at Time Management

Remember that there are certain conventions when it comes to e-mail. For example, to write in capital letters (upper case) is considered rude as it is akin to shouting. Beware of 'text-speak', that is to say using modern acronyms for messages where these might not be understood by the recipient. Essentially, the same attention to care and detail should be afforded to e-mail as to any other form of written communication.

How many e-mails a day do you send and receive (on average)?

On reflection, are there any strategies that you could employ that could make this valuable form of communication more effective?

What did you really do today? – A Fresh Look at Time Management

TOP TIPS

- Ensure that your details are only on circulation lists where absolutely necessary.
- Check your inbound messages at specific times only, *not* every time a new message comes in.
- Check your e-mail etiquette. For example, are you using the 'deal with it, delegate it, schedule it, file it, bin it' approach?
- Set up folders for your messages. Do not allow messages to sit in your 'in box' after receipt. If they cannot be deleted, dealt with or forwarded for action straight away, then ensure that they are moved to the appropriate folder.
- Investigate and make use of all of the features offered by your e-mail provider. Most people under-use these, and are sometime completely unaware of options that could save them a great deal of time.
- Make best use of the subject line. Appropriate use of this can sometimes negate the need to expand further, saving both you and the reader time.
- Work with those with who you correspond to create a positive e-mail culture, explaining any initiatives and sharing best practice.

LOCK IT IN

You should now stop reading and not continue any further until you have reflected upon you current e-mail practices and implemented any changes.

What did you really do today? – A Fresh Look at Time Management

Travel

In an increasingly busy world, it seems that most people spend more and more of their time travelling. Indeed, a daily commute of say an hour each way to and from work is not uncommon, and based on a 37.5 hour working week over 48 weeks of the year that equates to nearly 13 days per annum. Factor in a few delays and the occasional journey within the working day and you can quickly 'kiss goodbye' to the equivalent of three weeks.

Now of course time spent travelling is not necessarily wasted. Many enjoy their time at the wheel or on the train, and see it as a way of preparing for or winding down from a 'hard day's slog'. Maybe they listen to music and use the opportunity to relax or de-stress, or utilise the time constructively to think about or plan elements of their work. But for others travelling may be frustrating. Maybe by the time they arrive at work (or get home at night) their blood pressure is frequently raised from the experience, leaving them annoyed or bad-tempered?

Certainly I fall into the second category. I am told that there are roughly twice as many vehicles on the road now compared with when I started driving (and most of them seem to be heading in exactly the same direction as me!) yet the road network isn't so very different from 30 years ago. Likewise the UK population has risen by several million in the same period, with little evidence of a proportionate increase in other means of travel.

Another thing that intrigues me is that for most people, the 'traditional working day' hasn't changed much in generations either. What I mean by this is that the daily '9 'til 5' routine appears set in stone for millions of individuals, causing an obvious peak in human and vehicular traffic around those times. It's like more and more liquid being forced through the same size tube!

And this is where some aspects of modern working can be great. Employers offering staff the facility of flexi-time for example often discover higher levels of productivity overall. Obviously a few arrive earlier and finish later, in some cases 'banking hours' for that all-important extra day off every now and then. But importantly it allows people to *choose* how to work, and as well as giving individuals a feeling of empowerment (which in itself can be quite motivating), can reduce journey times if they opt to travel slightly outside of the usual 'rush hour'. It can also broaden the talent pool because flexi-time may mean that individuals who could otherwise not consider work due to fixed-time commitments are now able to do so, potentially benefitting both businesses and families alike.

For some the ultimate solution to travel issues is to work from home, and interestingly here there has been something of a shift in attitudes over recent years. Historically one *went to work* but with modern-day technology it is often not necessary to literally do so. With a suitable computer, broadband connection and telephone, many office workers don't really need to leave their homes on a daily basis at all, and could be as productive (if not more so) from the comfort of their living room. Furthermore, in many cases their customers would be none the wiser!

What did you really do today? – A Fresh Look at Time Management

Some of Britain's biggest companies are realising the benefits of this particular form of flexible working, and any fears of staff skiving off to pop to the shops or watch daytime television have been dis-proven time after time as studies consistently conclude that home-workers are *more* productive than their office-based counterparts. And quite apart from the productivity benefits there are environmental and potential health advantages too, to say nothing of the need for less costly office space. Now of course it is important that home-based workers don't become isolated from what is taking place within the organisation, and good communication and a management understanding of the need for 'involvement' as a tool for motivation is very important to ensure that the benefits don't wear off, but if these risks can be addressed then working from home could be the way forwards for many.

It may be that your employer won't allow working from home, either because they don't fully appreciate the concept or perhaps because the business model prevents it. In these cases perhaps there's an interim 'halfway house'. For example, would it be possible for you to work on that important report from home (where it will probably be quieter and you'll complete it in far less time), or could you start at 10.00am and finish at 6.00pm on one day a week without disrupting the efficient-running of the organisation? If the answer is still "no", might it be worth seeing what similar businesses are up to and if their working practices have changed in recent times?

Does your employer have initiatives to support flexible (and / or home) working? If so, what are they?

What did you really do today? – A Fresh Look at Time Management

If your employer doesn't offer any such initiatives, what do you think they *could* consider that might be of benefit?

So far we have considered changes to traditional working patterns and the availability of employer-supported schemes for more flexible working, but what if these are not available to you? What if you have to come into work and the only option is to start and finish at specific times? And what if there are no other modes of travel or alternative routes? Well, here are some thoughts for you.

If you travel to work by car, do you *have* to do so? Are there any alternative means of transport (bus, train, car-share etc.)? Do you always travel the same route? Have you reviewed it recently? Do you notice trends in traffic volumes, for example during school holidays or where you have been either earlier or later than usual? If you varied your routine in any way would it make the journey less arduous or quicker?

If you travel by public transport (e.g. bus or train) do you take something to do during the journey? Perhaps you could catch up by reading some of those circulars or draft something that you could finalise later? Maybe you're lucky enough to have a tablet or notebook PC that allows you to utilise your journey time effectively? Or maybe you could simply sit back and reflect on or plan your day, or even relax and '(re)charge your batteries'?

What did you really do today? – A Fresh Look at Time Management

I recall once being told by somebody who travelled by train that he simply couldn't do any work because it was always too noisy and overcrowded. His solution was to occasionally upgrade his ticket from Standard to First Class when he had important work to do (the relatively small extra financial cost being a tiny price to pay for the relative space and ambience that helped him concentrate). If you can't do this, does your train have a designated 'quiet carriage' in Standard Class? It may not be less crowded but it should be a little quieter!

Many of us are creatures of routine. Maybe there is an alternative service that you could use? Do you know? Have you checked?

Unless you can upgrade and work in relative seclusion, aim to use your public transport travel time for those tasks that don't get compromised too much by interruptions. Short-burst activities are usually the best, with informational or background and perhaps B2 or C types the wisest choices.

Many people have to travel during the working day, maybe journeying to appointments or to see clients. If this is you, do you try to group or cluster these together so that your focus is on a specific geographic area thus minimising down time? Do you aim to avoid the most congested routes at the busiest times? Do you use a Satnav or App on your phone that has real-time traffic updates and route options on it? (The relatively small outlay could be repaid very quickly).

Do you need to actually *go there* at all? Is your attendance at a meeting really necessary, or could you be briefed on what went on later? Could you participate via audio or video-conference instead? Would it be feasible to attend just part of whatever it is you're going to, rather than the whole event? Is your journey (and the timing of it) something that is essential or has it come about out of routine? Re-visit your priorities and ask yourself honestly.

Waiting time

I often wonder, if we added it all up, how much time we spend waiting for things to happen each week?

I would include within this category other people whose poor timekeeping impacts on our day, being kept on 'hold' whilst somebody looks for something, late public transport or deliveries, IT or technical issues (including equipment failures and slow-running software or hardware), queues for things, waiting for e-mail responses or replies to enquiries and so on.

Naturally some of these cannot be foreseen, though others are predictable and tend to happen on a fairly regular basis. Certainly in the case of the latter it might be wise to have a few short-duration things handy that could be slipped-in when opportunities present themselves. By their very nature these tasks are likely to be relatively low on your priority list, but nonetheless will have to be done at some point so could come off your to-do list at that point.

Make a list below of some of the delays that you encounter.

What did you really do today? – A Fresh Look at Time Management

Now list some of the short-duration relatively low priority activities or tasks that you do on a regular basis. These won't be time-critical, but will need to be completed.

TOP TIPS

- Take a close look at your routines. Ask *why* you travel at certain times or use certain routes.
- If there is the scope to work from home, see if this would be possible.
- If your employer offers the opportunity for flexible working, or if you can adjust your hours, consider whether you could use the time more productively.
- If you travel by public transport, take a few minutes to check any alternatives.
- If it is likely that you will be delayed or that you will have to wait for somebody, have something with you to do during the time.

LOCK IT IN

You should now stop reading for today. Spend some time reviewing your travel arrangements and reflect on how often you are kept waiting and how you could better use these periods.

What did you really do today? – A Fresh Look at Time Management

Core time management principles

We are coming towards the end of our 'journey' now, and when thinking about which tips and techniques to try, it is perhaps worth considering the following:

- It is important to 'connect to a purpose'. What is important to <u>you</u> and your organisation?
- Ensure that you put important things before less important things. (Sounds obvious doesn't it, but you'd be surprised just how many people have trouble evaluating 'importance')
- Manage your energy as part of your time planning
- Save energy by 'externalising' your to-do list (in other words – write it down). Don't be tempted to hold things in your head in the hope that you'll be able to 'juggle' and recall them all at the right moment
- Renewal and recovery is a responsibility and <u>not</u> an indulgence! You need to 'recharge your batteries' periodically
- Seek opportunities for inter-dependence rather than heroic independence

What did you really do today? – A Fresh Look at Time Management

Change and time management

One of the most challenging aspects in improving time management is the ability to change one's ways. Most agree that in order to progress it is necessary to alter our approach and methods periodically, but saying it and actually doing it are two different things.

The problem is that with change comes uncertainty. Perhaps yesterday wasn't perfect but it was nonetheless 'comfortable' and for many that is sufficient. We previously considered whether we are creatures of habit, and if we combine our natural tendency towards routine with our penchant for 'good enough' then it is not surprising that many resist change.

In fact it is widely known that the default is for most people to oppose change either actively or passively, and there is a recognised emotional response that cannot be countered by reason alone. The stages that are often experienced are as follows:

1. Relative 'stability' prior to the (announcement of) change
2. Inability to act due to surprise or shock
3. Denial or dis-belief
4. Anger as the reality of the situation takes hold
5. (Bargaining as some people try to resist what's happening)
6. Depression / feeling trapped when it is felt there is no scope for negotiation (doubt as to the future)
7. Testing of the 'new' (discovery)
8. Acceptance of the 'new' (integration)

Note that the length of each stage and its effect on the individual varies depending upon their personality, the nature of the change, whether multiple changes are occurring at the same time, and a number of other factors.

What did you really do today? – A Fresh Look at Time Management

It has often been said that people often fall into one of three distinct 'camps' when it comes to their initial reaction to change, and the first group are those who accept it without question. These represent a fairly small proportion of the population, sometimes choosing to just 'go with the flow' because it doesn't make a great deal of difference to them personally or alternatively because their nature is very passive. In the case of the latter there may well be anger or frustration, but this is likely to be directed inwardly rather than outwardly.

At the other end of the scale are those who are vehemently opposed. The numbers that react in this way will again be determined by the nature of the change and their individual personality, but no amount of logic is likely to 'win them round'. Their mind is made up and that is that! Managers often claim that large numbers of people respond in this way but in fact studies suggest that the reality is that the proportion is typically just one or two percent. However, where the change is carelessly or thoughtlessly implemented then the numbers can rise considerably.

But by far the largest proportion of people could be labelled 'believers but questioners'. This means that are naturally likely to be opposed to the initial announcement of the change(s), but that they can be convinced if the 'right argument' is put to them. 'Believers but questioners' are sceptical, but their scepticism can usually be attributed to one of just four reasons:

- Don't understand why / how
- No perceived benefits
- Fear of the unknown
- Fear of loss of power

Where their concerns are addressed correctly, all four sub-sections of this group can be easily won-over, but if the 'wrong' argument is used then no progress can be made. This is why there is often talk of 'selling' change or reference to people 'buying-in' to concepts. It's one of the oldest challenges in the world; give me a valid reason to do something and I might, but if you don't then I won't!

What did you really do today? – A Fresh Look at Time Management

So where somebody doesn't understand why or how, they need to be shown; either an explanation of the rationale or a demonstration will usually suffice and they will be on-side, but where they can't instantly see the benefits it may be necessary to adopt a WIIFM (What's In It For Me) approach.

If fear of the unknown exists, reassurance is the key, and where a fear of loss of power is present their confidence must again be re-built but this time with either proof that this isn't the case (or alternatives if it is).

At this point it is perhaps also worth reminding ourselves that people learn new things in different ways too, with some naturally likely to be more 'gung-ho' than others. Readers will no doubt be familiar with tried and tested development processes (the simplest being 'plan, do, review') and probably with the work of Honey and Mumford, Kolb, and others around preferred learning styles. What this means is that it is 'normal' to maybe not feel the same about something as your partner or neighbour. Likewise it may take longer to convince some people about a new concept than others, with the 'appeal' potentially differing from one individual to the next.

Suppose you gave a brand new mobile phone or tablet (that they had never seen before) to three different people. It is quite possible that one of them would open the box carefully and thoroughly read through the instruction manual whilst waiting for it to fully charge for the first time. The next might get it straight out, switch it on and start playing, adopting a trial and error style 'let's see' approach. The last person might track down somebody who had a similar model and ask them! There is no right or wrong. All might achieve the same result; they just *learned* differently.

What did you really do today? – A Fresh Look at Time Management

Improving your time management involves making changes. Note below how you typically learn new things. For example do you like to observe others, jump straight in etc.?

Reflect on a situation where you have been required to change something in your life. Maybe you moved house, bought a new car, or studied for a specific qualification etc. How did you feel before and during the period of change, and how did you feel afterwards?

TOP TIPS

- Re-visit the core time management principles. Reflect on those elements that are *really* important to you.
- Remember that for just about everybody, change equals uncertainty. However, some people respond better to change than others, and this can have a significant bearing on their effectiveness and general time management. Where an individual's genuine concerns can be established, steps can be taken to make the change(s) more palatable for them.
- People also 'learn' new things differently. Furthermore, some may need time to adjust, and the Kubler-Ross curve acknowledges that an initial dip in performance is natural for many following significant change.

LOCK IT IN

- You should now stop reading for today. The next section contains lots of time management tips, but before you consider these think about the core time management principles that are relevant to you and also how you (and those around you) typically react to change. Think too about your preferred method / style of learning as this will impact upon the techniques you adopt and how easily they will fit in with your life.

What did you really do today? – A Fresh Look at Time Management

Time management ideas and tips

Listed below are over 140 time management suggestions and tips. All of them have been proven to be relevant and effective for somebody, but not all of them will be appropriate for you.

Go through the list carefully, and against each put a tick if you are already doing it, a cross if you aren't (or if it genuinely wouldn't / couldn't work for you), and an asterisk / star if you think you might give it a try.

1. Make a time log so you know how you're currently spending your time, and how often and by what / who you're being interrupted.

2. Decide your mission and know what you want to get done today / this week / this month. Write your goals down and refer to them.

3. Put your list where you can see it. It's no good having a list in a book that you rarely open, or on a piece of equipment that you need to make an effort to get to!

4. If appropriate, and especially if you work in an open-plan environment, consider making your schedule visible so that other people can see it.

5. Make appointments with your tasks, so you have a plan of what you want do *when.*

6. Don't just use a list, use an urgency / importance grid as this helps with a purpose.

7. If it doesn't *need* doing, consider not doing it!

What did you really do today? – A Fresh Look at Time Management

8. Prioritise and have A, B1, B2, and C tasks. Aim to work on some of each every day.

9. Don't be tempted to keep things in your head. Capture (by writing it down) everything you have not yet done and need to do.

10. Have as many 'in trays' as you need, and no more! Have a 'to do' file, maybe organised A to Z or 1 to 31 as necessary.

11. Have a 'bring up / bring forward' file and or a 'waiting list'. Again you could use your A to Z or 1 to 31 for this.

12. Apply the Pareto Principle (a.k.a. the 80 / 20 rule) to what you are doing. Know what it is and try and focus on your most productive 20%.

13. Prepare before commencing something as this will increase your performance and productivity.

14. Use 'bite sized' chunks for larger projects and tasks that threaten to eat up large amounts of your time. Doing so makes the tasks seem less daunting, and also allows the smaller pieces to be either delegated or slotted into smaller gaps.

15. 'Sharpen the axe'. Take time out to improve your knowledge, skills and competencies. If you are constantly 'sawing at the tree', the axe will eventually become blunt and slow you down.

16. Find out what you are especially good at, and do more of it!

17. Conversely, identify where you would like to improve, and aim to reach this level so that it doesn't sabotage you.

18. Organise your schedule so that you have some 'prime time'. This should be time where you are uninterrupted, and can be utilised for tasks that require maximum concentration.

What did you really do today? – A Fresh Look at Time Management

19. Consider making use of quiet spaces / a quiet room occasionally. If your organisation doesn't have one, suggest it!

20. Book a meeting with an important person – you! This allows you to plan and set priorities.

21. Allow time in your diary every day where colleagues can speak with you. Over time, if you do this you will 'educate' them to disturb you only at these times. If you fail to let them know they will interrupt you whenever they want to!

22. 'Eat the frog!' This means getting the thing that is important to you that you really don't want to do done early. If you had to eat a frog today, eating it in the morning means that everything else this day will be easier! It is both satisfying, and takes worrying about it away.

23. Review your week ahead before you start on Monday morning. You will feel more confident and competent if you have a clear sense of your week's priorities, releasing energy for other things.

24. Take breaks! You will increase your efficiency and actually get more done if you take a recovery / renewal break every 90 to 120 minutes. This *is not* an indulgence, it's a responsibility!

25. Make your recovery breaks as effective as possible. Not all breaks have the same restorative power.

26. Pay attention to your personal energy cycle. You will have periods of enhanced and reduced energy across the day. Get to know them and where you can, schedule your work for appropriate points in the cycle. Plan difficult or mentally demanding tasks for periods of high energy, and less demanding ones in energy 'troughs'.

What did you really do today? – A Fresh Look at Time Management

27. Create your own deadlines but build in contingencies! Imagine you are called away for something and need to complete your tasks for then. Create your own (sensible) pressure before someone else does! Take control.

28. Clarify whether a deadline is based on need or want.

29. Re-negotiate deadlines (where possible) instead of rushing them.

30. Put off certain things that are not crucial to your agenda or job role so that you have the time to tackle the things that are.

31. Obey the law of enforced efficiency. There is seldom enough time to do everything, but there is usually time to do the most important things (so make sure you know what those things are).

32. Devote a regular period where you get through tasks that will not take any longer than two minutes each. This removes clutter from your to-do list and is quite motivating as things are quickly crossed off.

33. Build in 'response time'. When you make a list of things to complete, allow sufficient time to do it properly. And don't forget to also allow time for things that crop up unexpectedly.

34. Spend a regular period on important non-urgent tasks (B1 tasks). This is the proactive area of the urgency / importance matrix and will help create conditions that reduce the amount of 'fire-fighting' that will have to be done later.

35. Don't waste or tie up energy in negativity. If you are finding yourself with habitual complaints or toxic feelings, you need to make some changes. Don't marinate in negative energy!

What did you really do today? – A Fresh Look at Time Management

36. Spend regular time where you 'single touch' everything. Devote a period to fully dealing with, delegating, putting in the 'incubation' file, reference file, or bin whatever is in your 'in tray'. Your 'in tray' should not be a long-term resting place for items.

37. Don't confuse human beings and things! You can be efficient with things but you need to be effective with people. If you try to be efficient with people then you may be storing up problems that later will eat up more time than would have been taken had they been dealt with appropriately in the first place.

38. Aim to work in your zone of influence. Your zone of concern may be much bigger than your zone of influence, but if you expend energy outside your actual area of influence then you will expend it without productive return, and may further diminish your ability to work within (and ultimately expand) your zone of influence.

39. Make use of the speaker facility on your 'phone. Whilst you are waiting for a call to connect (or whilst on hold) this frees up your hands to be doing something else.

40. Ensure that you have programmed the most frequently dialled numbers as speed dials onto your handset. This saves having to look up the details every time and avoids misdialling.

41. Ensure that calls are diverted to you only when others are genuinely absent.

42. Try to clump similar things together. For example, make all of your outgoing calls within a specified period. Maybe refer to it as the 'calling people hour'.

43. At the beginning of a telephone conversation, state the purpose / goals of the call.

44. Call people just before lunch or at the end of the working day so that *they* want to keep the call brief.

45. Discuss specifics on the phone and get the other party to confirm to you by e-mail (then agree).

What did you really do today? – A Fresh Look at Time Management

46. Use voicemail selectively. Whilst one should not hide behind the answerphone, in many cases if callers do leave a message it means at least that you aren't interrupted from what you are doing. Furthermore you can call them back at a time convenient to you and with all of the relevant information to hand.

47. Resist 'drive by shootings'. Sometimes you have to say "yes", but the casual corridor conversation that leaves you with three more things to do should be resisted. If you had not been there at that moment would you have still ended up with the work or might somebody else have been approached?

48. Learn to say "no". Pay attention to the relationship and to the overall needs of the organisation, but where necessary have the courage to say "no". If you struggle with this, assertiveness training may help you.

49. Allow the world to unfold. Not everything is *your* responsibility personally. If you took a day off the world wouldn't stop, so take a break from managing all of it and just 'tend your own patch'!

50. Stop the self-criticism. Don't be too hard on yourself. There will always be room for improvement, but just get the job done, listen to feedback, learn from it and try to do it better next time.

51. Avoid wishful thinking as this can ruin any well-laid plan. Place realistic expectations on your projects and schedule room for problems when creating your time line.

52. Get rid of FOMO (Fear of Missing Out). You can't do everything!

53. Where you haven't achieved something within the original deadline, ask yourself "why"? Is the justification you've given the *real* one or didn't you really want to do it?

54. Start thinking in terms of 'opportunity cost'. By doing this I can't be doing something else. What are you missing out on by doing whatever you've scheduled in?

55. Educate yourself on time management. There is no definitive blueprint (you have to select what works best for you). So if you see or know of somebody who seems well organised and in control of their time, ask them how they do it.

56. Choose what to be perfect in. There are some areas of your life where you need to be an expert, and others where adequate is probably good enough. Know the difference and act accordingly!

57. Don't get depressed at bad judgement. Learn from it – it gives experience. Instead of saying "if only I had", say "next time I will"

58. Give up on perfection. Often 'good enough' is fine.

59. Delegate where you can. Create relationships of interdependency.

60. Delegate sensibly – not everything to one person.

61. Check your work – life balance. Do you live to work, or work to live?

62. Try to create a habit of finishing what you start. Whilst this is not always possible, having lots of unfinished tasks is both less efficient and de-motivating.

63. Drink coffee cautiously. Tea contains less caffeine and is healthier. Water is probably the most healthy of all, and is proven to aid concentration.

64. Remember that smoking and coffee breaks cost time, and probably take longer than you think. Both are also powerful stimulants, and to excess can be bad for you. That said, it is important to 'recharge' every so often so aim to take regular short healthy breaks instead.

65. Don't skip lunch! Okay, it may not be possible to stop for an hour, but 'working through' generally results in the onset of fatigue later in the day, slowing you both physically and mentally to the extent that you may actually end up getting *less* done overall.

66. Reward yourself for completing hard tasks. Maybe a chocolate bar or that cup of coffee or cigarette that you've been craving. But only once it's finished, only in moderation, and not too often!

67. It's good to relax and maybe have a night out every now and then but remember that excesses of alcohol can remain in your system the next morning and that, apart from being potentially dangerous if you drive or operate machinery, their effects can leave you feeling sluggish and can affect your capacity for working effectively.

68. Get some fresh air. In some environments the air quality may not be ideal. This might be especially true if you work in a room for hours with the door closed. Poor air quality can affect concentration levels and potentially one's health, so maybe open a window (or take a short walk) on a nice day.

69. Avoid attempting to do too much. We all have a 'saturation point' and whilst it's good to balance long-term projects with daily tasks, if there is simply too much to do then it may become difficult to make meaningful progress on anything.

70. More haste less speed! It may sound counter-intuitive, but sometimes if you 'pace yourself' (especially with complex work), by working at a slightly slower rate you will probably achieve the end result more quickly because you are not rushing and making silly mistakes.

71. Try and simplify what you can. Whatever you are doing, there is probably a simpler or more efficient way of doing it. Take a critical look at processes and try to think 'outside the box' for possible alternatives.

72. Commit a chunk of time for clearing your workspace and creating your work system. As you throw out old stuff you release energy, space and time for what is really important.

73. Once you have your system up and running, don't consider it frozen. Always be on the lookout for new ways of doing things, and see if your productivity is affected as a result. If all you ever do is all you've ever done, then all you'll ever have is all you've ever had!

What did you really do today? – A Fresh Look at Time Management

74. Don't save everything! Experts estimate that between 60% and 80% of what people file they never look at or refer to again. Learning what to save (and how to save it) and what to dispose of is essential in effective time management.

75. Focus on function. Decide the purpose of the area and organise accordingly.

76. Use a whiteboard in your workspace (but not an interactive one). Jot down things to do or ideas. It's cheap, accessible, visible, and adaptable.

77. Clear and sort. Look at the items around you. When did you last use them / work on them / refer to them? Remove those that shouldn't be there. Do the same with drawers, shelf tops etc.

78. Make your workspace attractive to you. It can be de-motivational if you dislike the area you work in.

79. Section your desk.

80. Work flexibly. Sometimes an hour before 9.00am can be twice as productive as an hour after 9.00am simply because of the level of interruptions (e.g. telephones ringing, other people being around etc.). Maybe work from home if this is feasible.

81. Consider the effect of music or the radio when working – for some it may be an aid to getting the job done, especially if the work is repetitive, but for others it could be a distraction.

82. Don't sit facing the door or window as it can be distracting.

83. If possible, try to locate yourself away from places where people tend to congregate as you may find yourself becoming drawn in to irrelevant conversation.

What did you really do today? – A Fresh Look at Time Management

84. If you are unfortunate enough to be located close to an item of equipment such as a printer or photocopier, never 'know' anything about it. If people think you do, you will become the source of information for every query, breakdown and paper jam for ever more!

85. Consider getting a 'do not disturb' sign for your desk. Subtle ... no, but effective ... yes!

86. If you have a visitor's chair close to your desk, make it uncomfortable or put something on it to deter visitors from sitting and lingering. If you can, remove it altogether.

87. Be strong! Switch your mobile off (or at least put it on silent) when you are working.

88. Have something that you want to do next. This focuses the mind and can help move the conversation along.

89. If others make appointments to see you, offer these at unusual times (e.g. 10.05am or 10.20am). This suggests that you are busy, generally improves punctuality, and implies that the meetings will be brief.

90. In one-to-one meetings, explain at the outset that you only have say five minutes. This will give you an excuse to leave or extend the duration as you wish.

91. When somebody is not leaving, stand up (and if needs be gradually move towards the door). If they don't get the hint, thank them for coming. If they still don't get the hint, shake them by the hand. And if they still show no signs of leaving, tell them you have to go now and say "goodbye".

92. Set time aside for colleagues and let them know when it is. If you don't then they'll interrupt you whenever *they* like.

93. Avoid impromptu meetings. These are very disruptive and are huge time thieves. Create a culture where all meetings must have at least a 24 hour lead time.

What did you really do today? – A Fresh Look at Time Management

94. Only have a meeting is there is a purpose, and avoid regular meetings just for the sake of having them.

95. Politely decline requests for you to attend meetings or lunches that aren't essential.

96. Always ensure that every meeting has an agenda, and that it is circulated in advance.

97. If you have been asked to attend a meeting, <u>ask</u> for the agenda if it looks as though one may not be forthcoming (and be prepared to say why you want it).

98. Start meetings on time! Don't wait for late-comers. If 12 people attend a meeting and it commences five minutes late, that's an hour of time that has been wasted collectively!

99. Consider holding meetings standing up! This happens in some countries abroad, the concept being that decisions are likely to take longer where attendees are seated and 'too comfortable'.

100. At meetings, abolish AOB (Any Other Business). Instead, why not have 'items for the next agenda'?

101. Respect others and their timetables by being punctual.

102. If you are unexpectedly delayed, let the other person know by sending a message or text.

103. Communicate clearly. Consider whether you are using the most effective or the most convenient medium for your message. When writing, write for the reader.

104. Don't be afraid to pick up the 'phone. Sometimes it's quicker!

105. Consider a speed-reading course.

What did you really do today? – A Fresh Look at Time Management

106. Get into the habit of reading with a highlighter pen in your hand so that you can quickly mark the passages that are of interest to you. Doing this can make them easier to locate next time.

107. Ask for feedback about your written work, and aim to incorporate as much of this as you can in future writing.

108. Make use of grammar and spell checkers, and ensure that any such aids are set to the correct defaults (language and style).

109. Spend an hour investigating keyboard short-cuts.

110. Don't sign-up to newsletters or circulation lists unless they are essential.

111. Back up your computer files periodically.

112. Use software that blocks unwanted applications or sites.

113. Consider using two monitors (or even two computers, e.g. desktop and laptop) as this can improve productivity as you won't need to switch back and forth between applications, just your displays.

114. Set reminders using electronic calendars.

115. Use your electronic calendar before somebody else fills it up!

116. Do you have e-mail or does it have you? Don't be tempted to go to your e-mail until you have got that important job finished. Control your own agenda.

117. Don't respond to e-mail by reflex. Exercise discrimination.

118. Don't leave unread e-mails in your 'in box'.

119. Put the onus on the *recipient* of the email to respond.

120. Don't automate e-mail. Some programs have a timer so that mail is checked on a certain schedule. Switch this feature off, and, depending on your needs, visit your 'in box' just three or four times a day at pre-defined times when you want to.

121. Do use an auto-responder if you are away from your office or on leave. It prevents 'chase-up' messages and gives the sender the opportunity to work it out for themselves or 'bother' somebody else.

122. Consider having two e-mail addresses; one for business essentials, and a second for non-essential messages (e.g. promotions / circulars etc.). This way your messages are effectively prioritised for you.

123. Set up folders for your e-mails. What you call them is entirely up to you, but do ensure that it makes them easy to locate when they are required and that it indicates their level of priority.

124. Consider e-mail training.

125. Don't lose ideas. Good ideas can come to you at any point during the day or night. Keep a notebook and make a note of them as soon as they pop into your head.

126. Maybe keep a pencil and paper by the side of your bed. Although it seems a shame, many people say that they wake up during the night and start thinking about work. If this happens then at least you can capture any thoughts for the morning and then go back to sleep happy that you won't forget about them.

127. Each week go to bed early, at least once! You are likely to be more productive, more cheerful and generally a nicer person to be with as a result.

128. Where appropriate, let people use their own imagination and initiative. It is motivating for them, and they will probably do it more quickly.

129. Set goals. Use the SMART system (Specific, Measurable, Achievable, Realistic and Timed), or the simpler 'Want it, Believe it, Write it down' approach.

What did you really do today? – A Fresh Look at Time Management

130. Don't file something that still needs your attention until you have recorded it in your time management system, otherwise you might overlook it (and any associated work that still needs to be completed). The same rule applies to both paper and e-mail documents.

131. Aim to have just one piece of paper (or the documents relating to just one task) on your desk at any one time.

132. Organise your paper files in a filing drawer or cabinet. (Do the same with your computer files, putting them into relevant folders).

133. Consider a 'rough filing' system unless it is likely that large numbers of documents will have to be located again quickly.

134. Want to improve your writing performance? It will probably be quicker to write it now and edit later, rather than try to do both simultaneously as you go along.

135. Make the most of situations where you can't do much else (e.g. reading paperwork on the bus / train).

136. Use checklists. If you need to do something repeatedly in the same manner, and especially if this might be delegated periodically, create a checklist so that one can quickly verify that all of the necessary elements are completed.

137. Be receptive to feedback from colleagues, and offer constructive comments to others. Ultimately 'two heads are better than one' and it might just save you time.

138. Consider planning (and giving out) tomorrow's work today. This allows those responsible for it time to think about how it might best be approached.

139. List the obstacles for you to effective time management. Remember to consider both 'internal' factors (those over which you have some control), and 'external' factors (those over which you don't).

140. Be sure about things – don't guess!

141. Clarity is crucial. Lack of clarity leads to lack of focus that often results in under-achievement and frustration.

142. Avoid procrastination. If you are a procrastinator, determine whether you are an 'arousal type', an 'avoider', or a 'decisional procrastinator', and act accordingly.

143. Remember, not everything works for everybody, so look at what might work for you.

144. Do it now! Start today!

145. Remember the three 'P's
    - Planning (if you don't have time for planning, you'd better find some)
    - Priorities (not everything is of equal importance; priorities are not constant, they must be re-evaluated)
    - Procrastination (the anti-Nike; just *don't* do it).

Please add any tips of your own below:

LOCK IT IN

You should now stop reading for today. Be clear about what you wish to put into practice, and make a note in your diary to read the final section of this book in approximately a month's time. Don't be tempted to read it beforehand as the intention is that it will act as a combined review and self-assessment of your progress.

What did you really do today? – A Fresh Look at Time Management

Time quotes

How people utilise their time is influenced by choices and pressures, and many have their own view as to what time management is all about.

Below are shown some time-related quotes attributed to some famous people.

"The bad news is that time flies. The good news is you're the pilot" (Michael Althsuler)

"Lost time is never found again" (John H. Augley)

"A committee is a group that keeps minutes and loses hours" (Milton Burle)

"Time is like money; the less you have of it to spare the further we make it go" (Josh Billings)

"We say we waste time but that is impossible. We waste ourselves" (Alice Bloch)

"Don't say you don't have enough time. You have exactly the same number of hours per day that were given to Helen Keller, Pasteur, Michaelangelo, Mother Teresa, Leonardo da Vinci, Thomas Jefferson, and Albert Einstein" (H. Jackson Brown)

"Doing a thing well is often a waste of time" (Robert Byrne)

"Time is the scarcest resource and unless it is managed nothing else can be managed" (Peter F. Drucker)

"All that really belongs to us is time; even he who has nothing else has that" (Baltasar Gracian)

"The future is something which everybody reaches at a rate of 60 minutes an hour, whatever he does, whoever he is" (C. S. Lewis)

"We must use time as a tool, not as a crutch" (John F. Kennedy)

What did you really do today? – A Fresh Look at Time Management

"The great French Marshall Lyautey once asked his gardener to plant a tree. The gardener objected that the tree was slow-growing and would not reach maturity for 100 years. The Marshall replied" in that case there's no time to lose; plant it this afternoon"" (John F. Kennedy)

"Minutes are worth more than money. Spend them wisely" (Thomas P. Murphy)

"Life offers two great gifts – time, and the ability to choose how we spend it. Planning is a process of choosing among those many options. If we do not choose to plan, then we choose to have others plan for us" (Richard I. Winword)

"Time is at once the most valuable and the most perishable of our possessions" (John Randolph)

"What may be done at any time will be done at no time" (Scottish Proverb)

Can you think of any more time-related quotes or wise-words relating to personal-effectiveness? If so, please note them below.

LOCK IT IN

You should now stop reading for today. Be clear about what you wish to put into practice, and make a note in your diary to read the final section of this book in approximately a month's time. Don't be tempted to read it beforehand as the intention is that it will act as a combined review and self-assessment of your progress.

One month later

Four or five weeks ago you should have completed the sixteenth section of this book, and hopefully gone away with lots of good intentions about how you were going to make positive changes to specific areas of your personal effectiveness.

Sufficient time should now have passed to be able to establish:

- Whether you have kept to those commitments
- Which are proving beneficial

If there have been any barriers to your plans, and it is likely that there will have been, you should consider whether these are self-imposed or whether others have impacted upon your ability to see them to fruition. In order to move forwards we often encounter obstacles in our way, and it may be necessary to think of new ways to address them so that we can reach our ultimate goal. With time management initiatives resistance often rubs-off from others, as in changing our ways it is likely that other people will become affected too. If they are apathetic then it simply makes the process of change for us that much harder! But anything that is worthwhile is likely to require some effort, so analyse the causes of any problems and seek ways of overcoming or avoiding them.

Re-visit the list of time management tips and make sure that you really have tried hard to incorporate those marked with an asterisk / star into your daily routines. If you haven't yet tried some that you were planning to, start doing them immediately, and if you began some and they have 'tailed off' ask yourself "why"? If you genuinely tried and they didn't work then fair enough, but if the effort given to them was not 100% then have another go!

What did you really do today? – A Fresh Look at Time Management

And finally, take another look at the personal objectives that you identified right at the start of the process by reviewing the grid on page nine. Have you seen improvements in the areas that you highlighted? If "yes" then great, but is there any more that you could do? And if not, ask "why" and think about what else might be done to assist you in this area.

Perfect time management is a bit like the end of the rainbow; it's always just that bit out of reach but we can sometimes get quite close! So keep 'chasing it' and review and allow your methods to evolve with time so that you stay as close as you can.

I hope you've enjoyed the journey ... so far!

LOCK IT IN

You should now stop reading for today, but if you have encountered any challenges in terms of making changes to your time management, you are advised to analyse what has happened and why. A sample grid is shown on the next page.

What did you really do today? – A Fresh Look at Time Management

Challenges and possible remedies

Period: **Sheet:**

Intention / Initiative	Barrier encountered	Nature of the problem	Possible remedy	Comments

What did you really do today? – A Fresh Look at Time Management

Glossary of terms

1 to 31 file: A method of filing where items are sorted and grouped based on *when* they need to be actioned.

Agenda: In the context of meetings, the term refers to a planned schedule of what should be happening and when.

Any other business (AOB): Frequently the last agenda item at meetings, the term refers to an open period where attendees can discuss issues that were not pre-advised to other participants. Most effective time managers agree that this is not a productive use of time, and that in most cases it should be replaced with 'items for the next meeting' instead.

Assertive behaviour: This type of behaviour is where an individual stands up for his / her own rights, but *without* violating the rights of others.

Believers but questioners: Natural sceptics in any change process whose resistance can usually be attributed to one of four underlying reasons.

Chair(person): A designated individual at meetings who ensures that protocols and best practice are adhered to, and that everything runs to time.

Chunking: An American term that refers to breaking a large task down in to smaller component parts. This makes them easier to schedule, and also less daunting.

Cost-Benefit analysis: The process of 'weighing up' the investment (in terms of money or time) against the potential 'payback'.

Delegation: Delegation is best defined as 'organised sharing of responsibility', the aim being to ensure that the most appropriate person undertakes each task / activity. As a minimum, considerations should include experience, knowledge, skills, motivation levels, and workload.

EOM: An acronym for e̲nd o̲f m̲essage that can be used in the subject line of an e-mail, indicating that there is nothing further to read.

Herzberg: Frederick Herzberg was a psychologist who developed a theory for motivation based on a set of 'hygiene factors' and 'motivators'.

What did you really do today? – A Fresh Look at Time Management

'Hot-desking': A term used in some modern workplaces where desk-space is shared / used by more than one individual.

Importance: A measure of the consequence(s) of *you* personally undertaking (or not undertaking) a task / activity, in relation to *your* role specifically.

Kubler-Ross curve: A recognised profile of the typical stages that people experience following significant change.

Maslow: Abraham Maslow was the theorist who identified five areas of need, believing that satisfying just the most basic (i.e. physiological and safety needs), is generally not enough to motivate people sufficiently.

Minutes (of meetings): A written record of what was discussed, and who it has been agreed will be responsible for specific actions moving forwards.

Motivation: This is the 'will to act', and is key in terms of productivity and / or performance.

'On-costs': The 'hidden' costs where human resource costs are being considered. Typically on-costs include National Insurance contributions, pension provision, training, sickness absence and holiday pay etc.

Opportunity cost: What *could* be done as an alternative to what you are doing (or planning to do).

Personal energy cycle: Your personal levels of physical and / or mental energy, and the effect that this may have on how quickly or effectively you are able to undertake specific tasks / activities.

Planner: Daily, weekly, or monthly planners are used to help people plan ahead. Whilst it is important to have a plan, it is also vital to ensure that there is some flexibility within them to allow for those unexpected crises.

'Prime time': Un-interrupted time which, if it is available to you, would be used for key activities.

Prioritising: The process of scheduling tasks / activities, and of deciding who should undertake them.

What did you really do today? – A Fresh Look at Time Management

Procrastination: Procrastination is the 'art' of putting things off! Common causes of procrastination include being disorganised, and being faced with less than appealing tasks. Whatever the cause, this can be a huge barrier to good time management.

'Rough' filing: A form of quick filing whereby instead of using strict alphabetical order, groupings are used. For example, maybe all the A's are put together, then all the B's etc.

SMART objectives / goals: A mnemonic or acronym that stands for Specific, Measurable, Achievable, Relevant and Timed.

Speed reading: A method of 'skimming' text that allows for the key points to be absorbed quickly.

Time log: A record of *exactly* how your time is spent, including details of all interruptions and unplanned activities.

Time thief: Somebody (or something) that wastes your time.

'To Do' list: A generic term that refers to a list of tasks / activities that need to be undertaken by you. It is good to attach some sort of priority to each.

'Two-minute' rule: A concept that acknowledges it is sometimes quicker to just do very short-duration tasks rather than schedule them in for later. Note that the rationale for this is that their scheduling and subsequent completion would actually take longer than the time taken to undertake them now.

Type 'A' tasks: Those that are both urgent and important, and which should be completed by you personally. By definition, these activities are reactive and can lead to high levels of pressure.

Type 'B1' tasks: Activities that can be scheduled in, but that are key to your role and thus should not really be delegated.

Type 'B2' tasks: These need completing fairly quickly, but because they are not crucial to your role, do not necessarily need to be done by you (unless you have some spare time available). Tasks of this nature should often be delegated, and if you find yourself routinely undertaking them personally, re-evaluate them critically.

Type 'C' tasks: By definition these are neither urgent nor important. They should not be on your 'to do' list at all, and of they are, should be left (at least for now).

Urgency: A measure of how soon something needs to be attended to.

WIIFM: What's in it for me?

WIIFY: What's in it for you?

What did you really do today? – A Fresh Look at Time Management

About the author

Peter Kennard is a professional trainer with his business based in the South West of England and has worked with organisations in the public, private, and voluntary sectors across the UK for almost two decades.

A Fellow of the Institute of Sales and Marketing Management he has engaged with clients at all levels, designing and delivering highly-effective bespoke and off-the-shelf training solutions.

With financial services and telecommunications management experience prior to specialising in learning and development, he has worked in most parts of the UK, travelling extensively at times for open courses, in-house programmes, and public speaking events.

More information about him and his company are available at:

Website: petekennardtraining.com

E-mail: petekennardtraining@mail.com

Phone: 0845 387 9876

What did you really do today? – A Fresh Look at Time Management